DANCING WITH JOY

DANCING WITH JOY

99 POEMS

EDITED BY
ROGER HOUSDEN

HARMONY BOOKS
NEW YORK

HARMONY BOOKS is a registered trademark and the Harmony Books
colophon is a trademark of Random House, Inc.

See page 197 for a complete list of permissions acknowledgments.

Library of Congress Cataloging-in-Publication Data
Dancing with joy : 99 poems / edited by Roger Housden.—1st ed.
p. cm.
Includes index.
1. Poetry—Collections.   I. Housden, Roger.
PN6101.D36   2007
808.81—dc22   2006015364

ISBN 978-0-307-34195-2

Printed in the United States of America

Design by Karen Minster

10 9 8 7 6 5 4 3 2 1

First Edition

CONTENTS

INTRODUCTION

Why all the embarrassment
about being happy?

asks Wendell Berry in his poem "Why," which you will find at the end of this collection. Why indeed! In the novel *Snow* by the Turkish writer Orhan Pamuk, one of the characters says to another,

> "You got drunk so you could resist the hidden happiness rising inside of you."

That's an original spin on the usual explanation, that people get drunk to drown their sorrows. What is it about happiness—not to mention joy—that prompts these authors to suggest it might be so daunting? Could it be that we live in such a difficult, tragic world that it can seem a betrayal or denial of our common darkness to jump for joy? That, in embracing happiness, we somehow turn our back on the sufferings of others—and, indeed, on our own sufferings—and so deservedly bring upon ourselves the retributions of guilt? This is precisely the question that Jack Gilbert addresses in his magnificent poem "A Brief for the Defense," and it is no accident that this poem features at the beginning of this book.

But there is something else: melancholy, despair, and depression are not only everywhere, an integral part of many people's experience, but they also have *cachet*. The demon of despair has always seemed more interesting than the angel of joy. *Melancholia* is weighty with meaning; it seems to be something of substance and conveys its substance onto its subject. If you have had a terrible childhood, you will be more likely to sell your autobiography than if you had an uneventful, happy one. Melancholy has always been equated with creativity and is commonly associated with art and artists, and, perhaps especially, with poets. Bob Dylan, in the recent film of his life by Martin Scorsese, says he has never had any interest in being happy. The hero of the novel *Snow* is a poet, a melancholic one, and someone says to him in earnest, and as a compliment, that

> "Only people who are very intelligent and very unhappy can write good poems."

Conventional wisdom tells us that nobody goes to heaven for having a good time. We genuinely think pain is virtuous, which is not surprising given that so many of us worship a crucified Savior. Suffering can indeed be a great purifier, a forger of character, no doubt about that; but joy can free us from our character altogether, at least for a time. It can take us out into the wide world beyond our own self-preoccupations. It can join us to the air and the trees, to other people, to cows and to stones and to the living spirit of humankind itself. It can join us to the china mug of tea in our own right hand.

This book exists to celebrate the many colors and freedoms of joy. Not that the poets represented here do not feel despair or loneliness—of course they do—but they have also known the rarer moments, or even whole periods, of grace, of inexplicable beauty, joy, and ecstatic insight; and from out of those times the most glorious poems have come—in resounding rebuttal of the speaker in *Snow*!

It must be said, though, that joy can even arise out of sadness itself:

> Sometimes from sorrow, for no reason,
> you sing . . .

says William Stafford in his poem "Cutting Loose." Or the Swede, Tomas Tranströmer, who in the poem "Allegro" says that

> After a black day, I play Haydn,
> and feel a little warmth in my hands.

Sometimes it is difficult even to tell the one from the other. In her poem "Thank You, My Fate," Anna Swir has this to say about making love:

> I don't know whether this is joy
> or sadness, I don't understand
> what I feel, I'm crying,

I'm crying . . .
I'm unworthy, how beautiful
my life.

Joy is an upwelling of life, of spirit, a blossoming of freedom. It is what we are here for. It is wholehearted, full-bodied, all-encompassing. In a moment of joy, you are no longer a kingdom divided—between right and wrong, this way or that way, should or shouldn't. And yet joy and melancholy exist on a spectrum and are not separate. This is why I have made the unlikely choice of including Pablo Neruda's poem "To Sadness" in a collection called *Dancing with Joy*. This book does not have the pink spin of candy floss. Its joy is substantial, even though it is often as light as air. And because the poems have weight as well as wings, they can afford to share space with a poem like this, in which Neruda reminds us that a surfeit of sunlight and honey can sometimes require its opposite to make sense of its beauty:

> *give me*
> *your black wing,*
> *sister sadness:*
> *I need the sapphire to be*
> *extinguished sometimes and the oblique*
> *mesh of the rain to fall,*
> *the weeping of the earth . . .*

Neruda's poem gives ballast, as well as an added lift, to all the joy surrounding it on the other pages.

Whereas melancholy can sometimes weigh heavy with

meaning, joy often seems to have no reason at all. It comes unbidden, and, as William Blake reminds us, leaves the same way. With no reason or purpose beyond itself, joy has no proper function in a utilitarian world. With no function, it has no intrinsic use. Joy is useless! It won't *get* us anywhere! Which may be another reason we tend to be wary of it. Joy exists in the present moment and has no plans for the future. It is not serious. When we are joyful, our plans and schemes and intentions all fly out of the window. When we are joyful, we have no future as such, because we are fully here in the present experience. You can only think about joy after it has come and gone. You can't train it to stay longer; nor can you work out how to repeat the experience. Joy, finally, is beyond our control, even if it might be true that we can learn how to become more prone to it. This is how Raymond Carver, in his poem "Happiness," puts it:

> *It comes on*
> *unexpectedly. And goes beyond, really,*
> *any early morning talk about it.*

Or as Mark Strand says in "Eating Poetry," inspired by an evening in a library in the company of poetry books,

> *I romp with joy in the bookish dark.*

Joy may indeed be useless, but it is also contagious. Any one of these pages may catch you alight. Anything, or nothing at all, can jump-start the tide of joy in our veins. For Wislawa Szymborska, it is a dream, or, in another of her poems, the joy of writing; for Robert Bly, being in the company of his ten-year-old son; for Stephen Dunn, coming home to his family; for Gerald Stern, it is dancing or a grapefruit at breakfast; for Kim Addonizio, it is a red dress; for Dorianne Laux, kissing; for Billy Collins, a cigarette; for Kabir, for Rumi, for Hafiz, it is spiritual joy. For Walt Whitman, it is friendship; for Wordsworth, solitude; for Keats, beauty. It is, finally, a sudden influx of life felt in all of its fullness, all of its transient beauty, its awakening joy.

Not that it is always easy or always a breeze to bear, as Denise Levertov suggests in "Matins":

> *Marvelous Truth, confront us*
> *at every turn . . .*
> *Thrust close your smile*
> *that we know you, terrible joy.*

Even so,

> *We must risk delight*

Jack Gilbert says, despite all our preoccupations with how difficult this life is. It is even our human, moral duty, he suggests. And once you can bear to see things for what they are, joy comes naturally—this, at least, is the view of Han Shan, the old Chinese poet-sage:

> *once you see through transience and illusion*
> *the joys of roaming free are wonderful indeed*

There are just four poems in *Dancing with Joy* that have appeared in previous collections of mine: "A Blessing" by James Wright, "Thank You, My Fate" by Anna Swir, and "Lines Composed a Few Miles Above Tintern Abbey" by William Wordsworth are all in my anthology *Risking Everything: 110 Poems of Love and Revelation;* "Thank You, My Fate" by Anna Swir is also to be found in *Ten Poems to Set You Free,* and "Ecstasy" by Hayden Carruth is in *Ten Poems to Last a Lifetime.* Try as I might to justify leaving them out, these poems would not lie down quietly. How can you have an anthology that goes by a name such as this, they clamored, and even think of our being absent? In any event, the context of this new anthology casts these poems in a somewhat different light. And in the case of the Wordsworth poem, it would have seemed a particular neglect given the inclusion of Billy Collins's hilarious "Lines Composed over Three Thousand Miles from Tintern Abbey," which cried out to have Wordsworth's original on the preceding page.

Risking Everything included a hundred and ten poems by a total of forty-eight poets. *Dancing with Joy* comprises ninety-nine poems by a total of sixty-nine poets. The range of poetic voice, then, has widened considerably here. *Dancing with Joy* has widened, too, in terms of time and space, spanning as it does a few of the English classical and Romantic poets, a Roman writer, some early Chinese poets, and poets from Turkey, Sweden, Poland, Russia, and France, as well as a strong representation of twentieth-century and contemporary American and English poets.

Even the experience and age range of the contributors has

widened. On the one hand, there is Stanley Kunitz, who was writing up until the day he died at age one hundred, and on the other is Erica Ehrenberg, a superb new voice who, at twenty-six, is having her work published here for the first time in book form.

All of which goes to suggest that there are, after all, many kinds of joy, to which neither age, nor era, nor continent can lay any exclusive claim. Joy, like suffering, is a quintessential human experience that comes unbidden; yet it is much rarer than its dark sister and is therefore more precious.

Which is all the more reason, I believe, for a volume like this that serves to catch the many forms of joy on the wing and hold them on the page as a mirror for our own moments of quiet or ecstatic abandon and that serves also as solace and inspiration for our own dark days, which, as we know, will always come. Finally, whatever else it is and in whatever form it shows up, joy is ever and always a gift; and it has been a gift indeed to me to have the opportunity to gather all these joys between two covers and send them out into the world.

DANCING WITH JOY

A BRIEF FOR THE DEFENSE

JACK GILBERT

Sorrow everywhere. Slaughter everywhere. If babies
are not starving someplace, they are starving
somewhere else. With flies in their nostrils.
But we enjoy our lives because that's what God wants.
Otherwise the mornings before summer dawn would not
be made so fine. The Bengal tiger would not
be fashioned so miraculously well. The poor women
at the fountain are laughing together between
the suffering they have known and the awfulness
in their future, smiling and laughing while somebody
in the village is very sick. There is laughter
every day in the terrible streets of Calcutta,
and the women laugh in the cages of Bombay.
If we deny our happiness, resist our satisfaction,
we lessen the importance of their deprivation.
We must risk delight. We can do without pleasure,
but not delight. Not enjoyment. We must have
the stubbornness to accept our gladness in the ruthless
furnace of this world. To make injustice the only
measure of our attention is to praise the Devil.
If the locomotive of the Lord runs us down,

we should give thanks that the end had magnitude.
We must admit there will be music despite everything.
We stand at the prow again of a small ship
anchored late at night in the tiny port
looking over to the sleeping island: the waterfront
is three shuttered cafés and one naked light burning.
To hear the faint sound of oars in the silence as a rowboat
comes slowly out and then goes back is truly worth
all the years of sorrow that are to come.

MINDFUL

MARY OLIVER

Every day
   I see or I hear
      something
         that more or less

kills me
   with delight,
      that leaves me
         like a needle

in the haystack
   of light.
      It is what I was born for—
         to look, to listen,

to lose myself
   inside this soft world—
      to instruct myself
         over and over

in joy,
    and acclamation.
        Nor am I talking
            about the exceptional,

the fearful, the dreadful,
    the very extravagant—
        but of the ordinary,
            the common, the very drab,

the daily presentations.
    Oh, good scholar,
        I say to myself,
            how can you help

but grow wise
    with such teachings
        as these—
            the untrimmable light

of the world,
    the ocean's shine,
        the prayers that are made
            out of grass?

HAPPINESS
Stephen Dunn

A state you dare not enter
   with hopes of staying,
quicksand in the marshes, and all

the roads leading to a castle
   that doesn't exist.
But there it is, as promised,

with its perfect bridge above
   the crocodiles,
and its doors forever open.

GRAMMAR

TONY HOAGLAND

Maxine, back from a weekend with her boyfriend,
smiles like a big cat and says
that she's a conjugated verb.
She's been doing the direct object
with a second person pronoun named Phil,
and when she walks into the room,
everybody turns:

some kind of light is coming from her head.
Even the geraniums look curious,
and the bees, if they were here, would buzz
suspiciously around her hair, looking
for the door in her corona.
We're all attracted to the perfume
of fermenting joy,

we've all tried to start a fire,
and one day maybe it will blaze up on its own.
In the meantime, she is the one today among us
most able to bear the idea of her own beauty,

and when we see it, what we do is natural:
we take our burned hands
out of our pockets,
and clap.

GOOD GOD, WHAT A NIGHT THAT WAS

Petronius Arbiter

Good God, what a night that was,
The bed was so soft, and how we clung,
Burning together, lying this way and that,
Our uncontrollable passions
Flowing through our mouths.
If only I could die that way,
I'd say goodbye to the business of living.

TRANSLATED BY KENNETH REXROTH

ECSTASY

Hayden Carruth

For years it was in sex and I thought
This was the most of it
                 so brief

                     a moment
or two of transport out of oneself
                      or
in music which lasted longer and filled me
with the exquisite wrenching agony
of the blues
              and now it is equally
transitory and obscure as I sit in my broken
chair that cats have shredded
by the stove on a winter night with wind and snow
howling outside and I imagine
the whole world at peace

                      at peace
and everyone comfortable and warm
the great pain assuaged
                     a moment
of the most shining and singular gratification.

YOUR LAUGHTER

PABLO NERUDA

Take bread away from me, if you wish,
take air away, but
do not take from me your laughter.

Do not take away the rose,
the lanceflower that you pluck,
the water that suddenly
bursts forth in your joy,
the sudden wave
of silver born in you.

My struggle is harsh and I come back
with eyes tired
at times from having seen
the unchanging earth,
but when your laughter enters
it rises to the sky seeking me
and it opens for me all
the doors of life.

My love, in the darkest
hour your laughter
opens, and if suddenly
you see my blood staining
the stones of the street,
laugh, because your laughter
will be for my hands
like a fresh sword.

Next to the sea in the autumn,
your laughter must raise
its foamy cascade,
and in the spring, love,
I want your laughter like
the flower I was waiting for,
the blue flower, the rose
of my echoing country.

Laugh at the night,
at the day, at the moon,
laugh at the twisted
streets of the island,
laugh at this clumsy
boy who loves you,
but when I open
my eyes and close them,

when my steps go,
when my steps return,
deny me bread, air,
light, spring,
but never your laughter
for I would die.

TRANSLATED BY DONALD WALSH

WHAT DO WOMEN WANT?

Kim Addonizio

I want a red dress.
I want it flimsy and cheap,
I want it too tight, I want to wear it
until someone tears it off me.
I want it sleeveless and backless,
this dress, so no one has to guess
what's underneath. I want to walk down
the street past Thrifty's and the hardware store
with all those keys glittering in the window,
past Mr. and Mrs. Wong selling day-old
donuts in their cafe, past the Guerra brothers
slinging pigs from the truck and onto the dolly,
hoisting the slick snouts over their shoulders.
I want to walk like I'm the only
woman on earth and I can have my pick.
I want that red dress bad.
I want it to confirm
your worst fears about me,
to show you how little I care about you
or anything except what
I want. When I find it, I'll pull that garment

from its hanger like I'm choosing a body
to carry me into this world, through
the birth-cries and the love-cries too,
and I'll wear it like bones, like skin,
it'll be the goddamned
dress they bury me in.

FROM BLOSSOMS

Li-Young Lee

From blossoms comes
this brown paper bag of peaches
we bought from the boy
at the bend in the road where we turned toward
signs painted *Peaches.*

From laden boughs, from hands,
from sweet fellowship in the bins,
comes nectar at the roadside, succulent
peaches we devour, dusty skin and all,
comes the familiar dust of summer, dust we eat.

O, to take what we love inside,
to carry within us an orchard, to eat
not only the skin, but the shade,
not only the sugar, but the days, to hold
the fruit in our hands, adore it, then bite into
the round jubilance of peach.

There are days we live
as if death were nowhere
in the background; from joy
to joy to joy, from wing to wing,
from blossom to blossom to
impossible blossom, to sweet impossible blossom.

PHOTOGRAPH

Lucille Clifton

my grandsons
spinning in their joy

universe
keep them turning   turning
black blurs against the window
of the world
for they are beautiful
and there is trouble coming
round and round and round

THE BEST CIGARETTE

BILLY COLLINS

There are many that I miss,
having sent my last one out of a car window
sparking along the road one night, years ago.

The heralded ones, of course:
after sex, the two glowing tips
now the lights of a single ship;
at the end of a long dinner
with more wine to come
and a smoke ring coasting into the chandelier;
or on a white beach,
holding one with fingers still wet from a swim.

How bittersweet these punctuations
of flame and gesture;
but the best were on those mornings
when I would have a little something going
in the typewriter,
the sun bright in the windows,
maybe some Berlioz on in the background.

I would go into the kitchen for coffee
and on the way back to the page,
curled in its roller,
I would light one up and feel
its dry rush mix with the dark taste of coffee.

Then I would be my own locomotive,
trailing behind me as I returned to work
little puffs of smoke,
indicators of progress,
signs of industry and thought,

the signal that told the nineteenth century
it was moving forward.
That was the best cigarette,
when I would steam into the study
full of vaporous hope
and stand there,
the big headlamp of my face
pointed down at all the words in parallel lines.

SONNETS TO ORPHEUS: IX

Rainer Maria Rilke

Only the man who has raised his strings
among the dark ghosts also
should feel his way toward
the endless praise.

Only he who has eaten poppy
with the dead, from their poppy,
will never lose even
his most delicate sound.

Even though images in the pool
seem so blurry:
grasp the main thing.

Only in the double kingdom, there
alone, will voices become
undying and tender.

Translated by Robert Bly

THE SUMMER DAY

MARY OLIVER

Who made the world?
Who made the swan, and the black bear?
Who made the grasshopper?
This grasshopper, I mean—
the one who has flung herself out of the grass,
the one who is eating sugar out of my hand,
who is moving her jaws back and forth instead of up and down—
who is gazing around with her enormous and complicated eyes.
Now she lifts her pale forearms and thoroughly washes her face.
Now she snaps her wings open, and floats away.
I don't know exactly what a prayer is.
I do know how to pay attention, how to fall down
into the grass, how to kneel down in the grass,
how to be idle and blessed, how to stroll through the fields,
which is what I have been doing all day.
Tell me, what else should I have done?
Doesn't everything die at last, and too soon?
Tell me, what is it you plan to do
with your one wild and precious life?

WHY I AM HAPPY

William Stafford

Now has come, an easy time. I let it
roll. There is a lake somewhere
so blue and far nobody owns it.
A wind comes by and a willow listens
gracefully.

I hear all this, every summer. I laugh
and cry for every turn of the world,
its terribly cold, innocent spin.
That lake stays blue and free; it goes
on and on.

And I know where it is.

OUR HEARTS SHOULD DO THIS MORE

Hafiz

I sit in the streets with the homeless

My clothes stained with the wine
From the vineyards the saints tend.

Light has painted all acts
The same color

So I sit around and laugh all day
With my friends.

At night if I feel a divine loneliness
I tear the doors off Love's mansion

And wrestle God onto the floor.

He becomes so pleased with Hafiz
And says,

"Our hearts should do this more."

TRANSLATED BY DANIEL LADINSKY

THE SWAN

KABIR

Swan, I'd like you to tell me your whole story!
Where you first appeared, and what dark sand you are going
      toward,
and where you sleep at night, and what you are looking for. . . .

It's morning, swan, wake up, climb in the air, follow me!
I know of a country that spiritual flatness does not control, nor
      constant depression,
and those alive are not afraid to die.
There wildflowers come up through the leafy floor,
and the fragrance of "I am he" floats on the wind.
There the bee of the heart stays deep inside the flower,
and cares for no other thing.

TRANSLATED BY ROBERT BLY

ADAM AND EVE IN THE GARDEN

John Milton

Both turned, and under the open sky adored
The God that made both sky, air, earth, and heaven,
Which they beheld, the moon's resplendent globe,
And starry pole: "Thou also mad'st the night,
Maker Omnipotent, and thou the day
Which we, in our appointed work employed,
Have finished, happy in our mutual help
And mutual love, the crown of all our bliss."
. . . .

This said unanimous, and other rites
Observing none, but adoration pure,
Which God likes best, into their inmost bower
Handed they went: and, eased the putting off
These troublesome disguises which we wear,
Straight side by side were laid: nor turned, I ween,
Adam from his fair spouse, nor Eve the rites
Mysterious of connubial love refused.
. . . .

Hail, wedded Love, mysterious law, true source
Of human offspring, sole propriety
In Paradise of all things common else!

By thee adulterous Lust was driven from men
Among the bestial herds to range; by thee,
Founded in reason, loyal, just, and pure,
Relations dear, and all the charities
Of father, son, and brother, first were known.
Far be it that I should write thee sin or blame,
Or think thee unbefitting holiest place,
Perpetual fountain of domestick sweets,
Whose bed is undefiled and chaste pronounced,
Present, or past, as saints and patriarchs used.
Here Love his golden shafts employs, here lights
His constant lamp, and waves his purple wings.

. . . .

These, lulled by nightingales, embracing slept,
And on their naked limbs the flowery roof
Showered roses, which the morn repaired. Sleep on,
Blest pair, and O! yet happiest, if ye seek
No happier state, and know to know no more.

FROM *PARADISE LOST,* BOOK IV

SABBATHS 2004: IV

Wendell Berry

(Jayber Crow in old age)

To think of gathering all
the sorrows of Port William
into myself, and so
sparing the others:
What freedom! What joy!

THE DANCING

GERALD STERN

In all these rotten shops, in all this broken furniture
and wrinkled ties and baseball trophies and coffee pots
I have never seen a postwar Philco
with the automatic eye
nor heard Ravel's "Bolero" the way I did
in 1945 in that tiny living room
on Beechwood Boulevard, nor danced as I did
then, my knives all flashing, my hair all streaming,
my mother red with laughter, my father cupping
his left hand under his armpit, doing the dance
of old Ukraine, the sound of his skin half drum,
half fart, the world at last a meadow,
the three of us whirling and singing, the three of us
screaming and falling, as if we were dying,
as if we could never stop—in 1945—
in Pittsburgh, beautiful filthy Pittsburgh, home
of the evil Mellons, 5,000 miles away
from the other dancing—in Poland and Germany—
oh God of mercy, oh wild God.

SABBATHS 1999: II

WENDELL BERRY

I dream of a quiet man
who explains nothing and defends
nothing, but only knows
where the rarest wildflowers
are blooming, and who goes,
and finds that he is smiling
not by his own will.

HAPPINESS

༄ JANE KENYON

There's just no accounting for happiness,
or the way it turns up like a prodigal
who comes back to the dust at your feet
having squandered a fortune far away.

And how can you not forgive?
You make a feast in honor of what
was lost, and take from its place the finest
garment, which you saved for an occasion
you could not imagine, and you weep night and day
to know that you were not abandoned,
that happiness saved its most extreme form
for you alone.

No, happiness is the uncle you never
knew about, who flies a single-engine plane
onto the grassy landing strip, hitchhikes
into town, and inquires at every door
until he finds you asleep midafternoon
as you so often are during the unmerciful
hours of your despair.

It comes to the monk in his cell.
It comes to the woman sweeping the street
with a birch broom, to the child
whose mother has passed out from drink.
It comes to the lover, to the dog chewing
a sock, to the pusher, to the basket maker,
and to the clerk stacking cans of carrots
in the night.
           It even comes to the boulder
in the perpetual shade of pine barrens,
to rain falling on the open sea,
to the wineglass, weary of holding wine.

THE SWAN

Mary Oliver

Across the wide waters
    something comes
        floating—a slim
        and delicate

ship, filled
    with white flowers—
        and it moves
        on its miraculous muscles

as though time didn't exist,
    as though bringing such gifts
        to the dry shore
        was a happiness

almost beyond bearing.
    And now it turns its dark eyes,
        it rearranges
        the clouds of its wings,

it trails
   an elaborate webbed foot,
      the color of charcoal.
         Soon it will be here.

Oh, what shall I do
   when that poppy-colored beak
      rests in my hand?
         Said Mrs. Blake of the poet:

I miss my husband's company—
   he is so often
      in paradise.
         Of course! the path to heaven

doesn't lie down in flat miles.
   It's in the imagination
      with which you perceive
         this world,

and the gestures
   with which you honor it.
      Oh, what will I do, what will I say, when those
         white wings
           touch the shore?

THANK YOU, MY FATE

Anna Swir

Great humility fills me,
great purity fills me,
I make love with my dear
as if I made love dying
as if I made love praying,
tears pour
over my arms and his arms.
I don't know whether this is joy
or sadness, I don't understand
what I feel, I'm crying,
I'm crying, it's humility
as if I were dead,
gratitude, I thank you, my fate,
I'm unworthy, how beautiful
my life.

TRANSLATED BY CZESLAW MILOSZ
AND LEONARD NATHAN

LINES COMPOSED A FEW MILES ABOVE TINTERN ABBEY

WILLIAM WORDSWORTH *(Excerpt)*

And I have felt
A presence that disturbs me with the joy
Of elevated thoughts; a sense sublime
Of something far more deeply interfused,
Whose dwelling is the light of the setting suns,
And the round ocean and the living air,
And the blue sky, and in the mind of man,
A motion and a spirit, that impels
All thinking things, all objects of all thought,
And rolls through all things.

LINES COMPOSED OVER THREE THOUSAND MILES FROM TINTERN ABBEY

BILLY COLLINS

I was here before, a long time ago,
and now I am here again
is an observation that occurs in poetry
as frequently as rain occurs in life.

The fellow may be gazing
over an English landscape,
hillsides dotted with sheep,
a row of tall trees topping the downs,

or he could be moping through the shadows
of a dark Bavarian forest,
a wedge of cheese and a volume of fairy tales
tucked into his rucksack.

But the feeling is always the same.
It was better the first time.
This time is not nearly as good.
I'm not feeling as chipper as I did back then.

Something is always missing—
swans, a glint on the surface of a lake,
some minor but essential touch.
Or the quality of things has diminished.

The sky was a deeper, more dimensional blue,
clouds were more cathedral-like,
and water rushed over rock
with greater effervescence.

From our chairs we have watched
the poor author in his waistcoat
as he recalls the dizzying icebergs of childhood
and mills around in a field of weeds.

We have heard the poets long dead
declaim their dying
from a promontory, a riverbank,
next to a haycock, within a copse.

We have listened to their dismay,
the kind that issues from poems
the way water issues forth from hoses,
the way the match always gives its little speech on fire.

And when we put down the book at last,
lean back, close our eyes,
stinging with print,
and slip in the bookmark of sleep,

we will be schooled enough to know
that when we wake up
a little before dinner
things will not be nearly as good as they once were.

Something will be missing
from this long, coffin-shaped room,
the walls and windows now
only two different shades of gray,

the glossy gardenia drooping
in its chipped terra-cotta pot.
And on the floor, shoes, socks,
the browning core of an apple.

Nothing will be as it was
a few hours ago, back in the glorious past
before our naps, back in that Golden Age
that drew to a close sometime shortly after lunch.

EATING POETRY

MARK STRAND

Ink runs from the corners of my mouth.
There is no happiness like mine.
I have been eating poetry.

The librarian does not believe what she sees.
Her eyes are sad
and she walks with her hands in her dress.

The poems are gone.
The light is dim.
The dogs are on the basement stairs and coming up.

Their eyeballs roll,
their blond legs burn like brush.
The poor librarian begins to stamp her feet and weep.

She does not understand.
When I get on my knees and lick her hand,
she screams.

I am a new man.
I snarl at her and bark.
I romp with joy in the bookish dark.

THAT CITY THAT I HAVE LOVED

Anna Akhmatova

That city that I have loved since I was a child
seemed to me today
in its December stillness
to be my squandered inheritance.

Everything that was handed to me spontaneously,
was so easy to give away:
the soul's burning heat, the sounds of prayer,
and the grace of the first song—

all, all carried away in transparent smoke,
turned to ash in the depths of the mirrors . . .
and now a noseless violinist
strikes up a tune from the irrevocable past.

With the curiosity of a foreigner
captivated by everything new
I listened to my Mother Tongue
and watched the sledges race.

Happiness blew in my face
with a wild freshness and force,
as though an eternally dear friend
accompanied me onto the steps.

TRANSLATED BY RICHARD MCKANE

FOR ANGELA

Margaret Menges

Angela's coming for dinner, he said and
he bought the card with flowers and red hearts
flashing in circles.
He set the card under the rose light
on the dining room table,
next to the bills and the junk mail
piled there in the daily hubbub
which we promptly cleared away
      because
Angela, Angela's coming, he said,
and it made me laugh to remember
and I thought it'd be swell to have a theme,
like a national holiday for young love, so
we had Angel-hair pasta and Angel food cake,
white and full of air, whipped cream
and strawberries redder than roses and
blood and fairy-tale apples.
Angela, Angela . . . she arrived like the
Fourth of July and sat at the
end of the table, staring into
the blue eyes of the boy I've known forever.

FOR MY SON, NOAH, TEN YEARS OLD

~ ROBERT BLY

Night and day arrive, and day after day goes by,
and what is old remains old, and what is young
      remains young, and grows old,
and the lumber pile does not grow younger,
      nor the weathered two by fours lose their darkness,
but the old tree goes on, the barn stands without help
      so many years,
the advocate of darkness and night is not lost.

The horse swings on one leg, steps, and turns,
the chicken flapping claws onto the roost, its wings
      whelping and whalloping,
but what is primitive is not to be shot out into the night
      and the dark.
And slowly the kind man comes closer, loses his rage,
      sits down at table.

So I am proud only of those days that pass in
      undivided tenderness,
when you sit drawing, or making books, stapled,
      with messages to the world . . .

or coloring a man with fire coming out of his hair.
Or we sit at a table, with small tea carefully poured;
so we pass our time together, calm and delighted.

WELCOME MORNING

ANNE SEXTON

There is joy
in all:
in the hair I brush each morning,
in the Cannon towel, newly washed,
that I rub my body with each morning,
in the chapel of eggs I cook
each morning,
in the outcry from the kettle
that heats my coffee
each morning,
in the spoon and the chair
that cry "hello there, Anne"
each morning,
in the godhead of the table
that I set my silver, plate, cup upon
each morning.

All this is God,
right here in my pea-green house
each morning
and I mean,

though often forget,
to give thanks
to faint down by the kitchen table
in a prayer of rejoicing
as the holy birds at the kitchen window
peck into their marriage of seeds.

So while I think of it,
let me paint a thank-you on my palm
for this God, this laughter of the morning,
lest it go unspoken.

The Joy that isn't shared, I've heard,
dies young.

ALL THE EARTH, ALL THE AIR
Theodore Roethke

1

I stand with standing stones.
The stones stay where they are.
The twiny winders wind;
The little fishes move.
A ripple wakes the pond.

2

This joy's my fall. I am!—
A man rich as a cat,
A cat in the fork of a tree,
When she shakes out her hair.
I think of that, and laugh.

3

All innocence and wit,
She keeps my wishes warm;
When, easy as a beast,
She steps along the street,
I start to leave myself.

4

The truly beautiful,
Their bodies cannot lie:
The blossom stings the bee.
The ground needs the abyss,
Say the stones, say the fish.

5

A field recedes in sleep.
Where are the dead? Before me
Floats a single star.
A tree glides with the moon.
The field is mine! Is mine!

6

In a lurking-place I lurk,
One with the sullen dark.
What's hell but a cold heart?
But who, faced with her face,
Would not rejoice?

MAGNIFICENT THE MORNING WAS

WILLIAM WORDSWORTH *(Excerpt)*

                    Magnificent
The morning was, a memorable pomp,
More glorious than I ever had beheld.
The sea was laughing at a distance; all
The solid mountains were as bright as clouds,
Grain-tinctured, drench'd in empyrean light;
And in the meadows and the lower grounds,
Was all the sweetness of a common dawn—
Dews, vapours, and the melody of birds,
And labourers going forth into the fields.
Ah! Need I say, dear friend, that to the brim
My heart was full? I made no vows, but vows
Were then made for me: bond unknown to me
Was given, that I should be—else sinning greatly—
A dedicated spirit. On I walked
In blessedness, which even yet remains.

                    FROM "THE PRELUDE"

I SING THE BODY ELECTRIC

WALT WHITMAN *(Excerpt)*

4

I have perceiv'd that to be with those I like is enough,
To stop in company with the rest at evening is enough,
To be surrounded by beautiful, curious, breathing,
    laughing flesh is enough,
To pass among them, or touch any one, or rest my arm
    ever so lightly round his or her neck for a moment—
    what is this, then?
I do not ask any more delight—I swim in it, as in a sea.

There is something in staying close to men and women,
    and looking on them, and in the contact and odor of
    them, that pleases the soul well,
All things please the soul, but these please the soul well.

SEA-FEVER

John Masefield

I must go down to the seas again, to the lonely sea
  and the sky,
And all I ask is a tall ship and a star to steer her by,
And the wheel's kick and the wind's song and the white sail's
  shaking,
And a grey mist on the sea's face, and a grey dawn breaking.

I must go down to the seas again, for the call of the running
  tide
Is a wild call and a clear call that may not be denied;
And all I ask is a windy day with the white clouds flying,
And the flung spray and the blown spume, and the sea-gulls
  crying.

I must go down to the seas again, to the vagrant gypsy life,
To the gull's way and the whale's way, where the wind's like a
  whetted knife;
And all I ask is a merry yarn from a laughing fellow-rover,
And quiet sleep and a sweet dream when the long trick's over.

THE JOYS THAT STING

C. S. Lewis

Oh do not die, says Donne, *for I shall hate*
All women so. How false the sentence rings.
Women? But in a life made desolate
It is the joys once shared that have the stings.
To take the old walks alone, or not at all,
To order one pint where I ordered two,
To think of, and then not to make, the small
Time-honoured joke (senseless to all but you);
To laugh (oh, one'll laugh), to talk upon
Themes we talked upon when you were there,
To make some poor pretence of going on,
Be kind to one's old friends, and seem to care,
While no one (O God) through the years will say
The simplest common word in just your way.

SURPRISED BY JOY

WILLIAM WORDSWORTH *(Excerpt)*

Surprised by joy—impatient as the Wind
I turned to share the transport—Oh! with whom
But Thee, deep buried in the silent tomb,
That spot which no vicissitude can find?
Love, faithful love, recalled thee to my mind—
But how could I forget thee? Through what power,
Even for the least division of an hour,
Have I been so beguiled as to be blind
To my most grievous loss?—That thought's return
Was the worst pang that sorrow ever bore
Save one, one only, when I stood forlorn,
Knowing my heart's best treasure was no more;
That neither present time, nor years unborn,
Could to my sight that heavenly face restore.

FROM "THE PRELUDE"

A DIALOGUE OF SELF AND SOUL

W. B. YEATS *(Excerpt)*

I am content to follow to its source
Every event in action or in thought;
Measure the lot; forgive myself the lot!
When such as I cast out remorse
So great a sweetness flows into the breast
We must laugh and we must sing,
We are blest by everything,
Everything we look upon is blest.

MY TRUE HOME IS COLD MOUNTAIN

HAN SHAN *(Excerpt)*

My true home is Cold Mountain . . .

The Tientai Mountains are my home
mist-shrouded cloud paths keep guests away
thousand-meter cliffs make hiding easy
above a rocky ledge among ten thousand streams
with bark hat and wooden clogs I walk along the banks
with hemp robe and pigweed staff I circumambulate the peaks
once you see through transience and illusion
the joys of roaming free are wonderful indeed

TRANSLATED BY RED PINE

THE ENQUIRY

ANNE FINCH *(Excerpt)*

I've searcht the barren World, but cannot find
A Happiness for an Immortal Mind.
Honours, Delights and Riches have all spent
Their Smiles in vain, to give my *Thoughts Content,*
The Joys they yield, but for a Moment last,
And shrink to nothing when they're close embrac't,
They never satisfy, but feed desire,
And bring fresh Fuel to a restless Fire
What's one poor drop to him that almost bursts
With fierce desires, and for an Ocean thirsts.
My Mind can hold both the rich *Indy's* store,
And find it self, as empty as before.
The Treasures Earth throws in their purpose miss,
Swallow'd and lost in that immense Abyss.
I've look'd o'er all the Riches Earth can shew
All that it Promises, but gives to few:
And still some Intellectual Good I want,
Some Happiness this World can never grant.

Hence mighty God my Thoughts ascend to Thee,
The spring of Good, and Man's Felicity.

'Tis only they Immensity can fill
The thirsty Soul's vast and immortal Will.
This single Thought, that all Earth's Joys at Death
Will end, and cease for ever with my Breath,
Quite chills my Love, and lessens my Esteem,
And makes a Kingdom but a trifle seem.
I find my Soul's misplac'd, it longs to see
Some higher Good, some fix'd Felicity,
Which it despairs to met with, but in thee
I'm blest with Faculties to entertain
Thy self, and sure thou mad'st them not in vain.
And as I can, so I desire to be
Made happy only in Enjoying thee;
My Wishes else unsatisfy'd return,
And make me all my lost Endeavours mourn.

From *Miscellanea Sacra*, 1696, one of six poems that have been overlooked by scholars and that are clearly by Anne Finch. See Annotated Chronology, Entry # 63 (1696).

BATHING THE NEW BORN

Sharon Olds

I love with an almost fearful love
to remember the first baths I gave him,
our second child, so I knew what to do.
I laid the little torso along
my left forearm, nape of the neck
in the crook of my elbow, hips nearly as
small as a least tern's tail
against my wrist, thigh held loosely
in the loop of thumb and forefinger, the
sign that means exactly right. I'd soap him,
the violet, cold feet, the scrotum
wrinkled as a waved whelk, the chest,
hands, clavicles, throat, gummy
furze of the scalp. When I got him too soapy he'd
slide in my grip like an armful of buttered
noodles, but I'd hold him not too tight,
I felt that I was good for him,
I'd tell him about his wonderful body
and the wonderful soap, and he'd look up at me,
one week old, his eyes still wide
and apprehensive. I love that time

when you croon and croon to them, you can see
the calm slowly entering them, you can
sense it in your clasping hand,
the loose spine relaxing against
the muscle of your forearm, you feel the fear
leaving their bodies, he lay in the blue
oval plastic baby tub and
looked at me in wonder and began to
move his silky limbs at will in the water.

I TASTE A LIQUOR NEVER BREWED

EMILY DICKINSON

I taste a liquor never brewed,
From tankards scooped in pearl;
Not all the vats upon the Rhine
Yield such an alcohol!

Inebriate of air am I,
And debauchee of dew,
Reeling, through endless summer days,
From inns of molten blue.

When landlords turn the drunken bee
Out of the foxglove's door,
When butterflies renounce their drams,
I shall but drink the more!

Till seraphs swing their snowy hats,
And saints to windows run,
To see the little tippler
Leaning against the sun!

TAKING OFF EMILY DICKINSON'S CLOTHES

BILLY COLLINS

First, her tippet made of tulle,
easily lifted off her shoulders and laid
on the back of a wooden chair.

And her bonnet,
the bow undone with a light forward pull.

Then the long white dress, a more
complicated matter with mother-of-pearl
buttons down the back,
so tiny and numerous that it takes forever
before my hands can part the fabric,
like a swimmer's dividing water,
and slip inside.

You will want to know
that she was standing
by an open window in an upstairs bedroom,
motionless, a little wide-eyed,

looking out at the orchard below,
the white dress puddled at her feet
on the wide-board, hardwood floor.

The complexity of women's undergarments
in nineteenth-century America
is not to be waved off,
and I proceeded like a polar explorer
through clips, clasps, and moorings,
catches, straps, and whalebone stays,
sailing toward the iceberg of her nakedness.

Later, I wrote in a notebook
it was like riding a swan into the night,
but, of course, I cannot tell you everything—
the way she closed her eyes to the orchard,
how her hair tumbled free of its pins,
how there were sudden dashes
whenever we spoke.

What I can tell you is
it was terribly quiet in Amherst
that Sabbath afternoon,
nothing but a carriage passing the house,
a fly buzzing in a windowpane.

So I could plainly hear her inhale
when I undid the very top
hook-and-eye fastener of her corset

and I could hear her sigh when finally it was unloosed,
the way some readers sigh when they realize
that Hope has feathers,
that Reason is a plank,
that Life is a loaded gun
that looks right at you with a yellow eye.

'TIS SO MUCH JOY!

EMILY DICKINSON

'Tis so much joy! 'Tis so much joy!
If I should fail, what poverty!
And yet, as poor as I,
Have ventured all upon a throw!
Have gained! Yes! Hesitated so—
This side the Victory!

Life is but Life! And Death, but Death!
Bliss is, but Bliss, and Breath but Breath!
And if indeed I fail,
At least, to know the worst, is sweet!
Defeat means nothing *but* Defeat,
No drearier, can befall!

And if I gain! Oh Gun at Sea!
Oh Bells, that in the Steeples be!
At first, repeat it slow!
For Heaven is a different thing,
Conjectured, and waked sudden in—
And might extinguish me!

MIND WANTING MORE

Holly Hughes

Only a beige slat of sun
above the horizon, like a shade pulled
not quite down. Otherwise,
clouds. Sea rippled here and
there. Birds reluctant to fly.
The mind wants a shaft of sun to
stir the grey porridge of clouds,
an osprey to stitch the sea to sky
with its barred wings, some dramatic
music: a symphony, perhaps
a Chinese gong.

But the mind always
wants more than it has—
one more bright day of sun,
one more clear night in bed
with the moon; one more hour
to get the words right; one
more chance for the heart in hiding

to emerge from its thicket
in dried grasses—as if this quiet day
with its tentative light weren't enough,
as if joy weren't strewn all around.

BUT YOU WHO ARE SO HAPPY HERE

Dante Alighieri *(Excerpt)*

"But you who are so happy here, tell me:
     do you aspire to a more profound
     insight, or a greater ecstasy?"
She smiled a little, as did the shades beside her;
     then answered with such gladness that her whole
     being seemed to glow with love's first fire:
"Brother, God's generosity itself
     calms our will, and makes us want no more
     than what we have, and long for nothing else.
If we desired any greater bliss,
     we would not be in harmony with Him
     whose love assigns us to a lower place.
The essence of this joy is that we all
     have given up our personal desires
     so that our will is merged with God's own will.
Therefore our rank in heaven, from height to height,
     is just as dear to each particular soul
     as to the Master who appointed it.

In His will is our peace: it is the sea
    into which all currents and all streams
    empty themselves, for all eternity."

TRANSLATED BY STEPHEN MITCHELL
FROM *PARADISO*, CANTO III

THE JOY OF WRITING

Wislawa Szymborska *(Excerpt)*

Why does this written doe bound through these written woods?
For a drink of written water from a spring
whose surface will xerox her soft muzzle?
Why does she lift her head; does she hear something?
Perched on four slim legs borrowed from the truth,
she pricks up her ears beneath my fingertips.
Silence—this word also rustles across the page
and parts the boughs
that have sprouted from the word "woods."

Lying in wait, set to pounce on the blank page,
are letters up to no good,
clutches of clauses so subordinate
they'll never let her get away.

Each drop of ink contains a fair supply
of hunters, equipped with squinting eyes behind their sights,
prepared to swarm the sloping pen at any moment,
surround the doe, and slowly aim their guns.

TRANSLATED BY STANISLAW BARAŃCZAK
AND CLARE CAVANAGH

HAPPINESS

RAYMOND CARVER

So early it's still almost dark out.
I'm near the window with coffee,
and the usual early morning stuff
that passes for thought.
When I see the boy and his friend
walking up the road
to deliver the newspaper.
They wear caps and sweaters,
and one boy has a bag over his shoulder.
They are so happy
they aren't saying anything, these boys.
I think if they could, they would take
each other's arm.
It's early in the morning,
and they are doing this thing together.
They come on, slowly.
The sky is taking on light,
though the moon still hangs pale over the water.
Such beauty that for a minute
death and ambition, even love,
doesn't enter into this.

Happiness. It comes on
unexpectedly. And goes beyond, really,
any early morning talk about it.

TO SADNESS

Pablo Neruda

Sadness, I need
your black wing,
so much sun, so much honey in the topaz,
each ray smiles
in the meadow
and everything is round light on all sides of me,
everything is an electric bee in the heights.
And so
give me
your black wing,
sister sadness:
I need the sapphire to be
extinguished sometimes and the oblique
mesh of the rain to fall,
the weeping of the earth:
I want
that shattered beam in the estuary,
the vast house in darkness,
and my mother
searching

for paraffin
and filling the lamp
until it gave not light but a sigh.

The night wasn't born.

The day was sliding
toward its provincial graveyard,
and between the bread and the shadow
I remember
myself
in the window
looking out at what didn't exist,
what wasn't happening,
and a black wing of water that came
over that heart which there perhaps
I forgot forever, in the window.

Now I miss
the black light.

Give me your slow blood,
cold
rain,
give me your astonished flight!
Give me back
the key
of the door that was shut,
destroyed.

For a moment, for
a short lifetime,
take the light from me and let me
feel myself
lost and miserable,
trembling among the threads
of twilight,
receiving into my soul
the trembling
hands
of
the
rain.

TRANSLATED BY STEPHEN MITCHELL

SALT HEART

JANE HIRSHFIELD

I was tired,
half sleeping in the sun.
A single bee
delved the lavender nearby,
and beyond the fence,
a trowel's shoulder knocked a white stone.
Soon, the ringing stopped.
And from somewhere,
a quiet voice said the one word.
Surely a command,
though it seemed more a question,
a wondering perhaps—"What about joy?"
So long it had been forgotten,
even the thought raised surprise.
But however briefly, there,
in the untuned devotions of bee
and the lavender fragrance,
the murmur of better and worse was unimportant.
From next door, the sound of raking,
and neither courage nor cowardice mattered.

Failure—uncountable failure—did not matter.
Soon enough that gate swung closed,
the world turned back to heart-salt
of wanting, heart-salts of will and grief.
My friend would continue dying, at last
only exhausted, even his wrists thinned with pain.
The river Suffering would take what it
wished of him, then go. And I would stay
and drink on, as the living do, until the rest
would enter into that water—the lavender swept in,
the bee, the swallowed labors of my neighbor.
The ordinary moment swept in, whatever it drowsily holds.
I begin to believe the only sin is distance, refusal.
All others stemming from this. Then come.
Rivers, come. Irrevocable futures, come. Come even joy.
Even now, even here, and though it vanish like him.

KISSING AGAIN

Dorianne Laux

Kissing again, after a long drought of not kissing—
    too many kids,
bills, windows

needing repair. Sex, yes, though squeezed in between
    the minor depths
of anger, despair—

standing up amid the laundry or fumbling onto
    the strip of rug between
the coffee table

and the couch. Quick, furtive, like birds, a dance on
    the wing, but no
time for kissing,

the luxuriant tonguing of another spongy tongue,
    the deft flicking and
feral sucking,

that prolonged lapping that makes a smooth stone
    of the brain.
To be lost in it,

your body tumbled in sea waves, no up or down,
    salt and the
liquid swells

set in motion by the moon, by a tremor in Istanbul,
    the waft of a moth
wing

before it plows into a halo of light, a deep lustrous
    kiss that lasts
minutes, blossoms

into what feels like days, fields of tulips glossy with dew, low
    purple
clouds piling in

beneath the distant arch of a bridge. One after another
    they storm
your lips, each kiss

a caress, autonomous and alive, spilling into each other, streams
into creeks into rivers

that grunt and break upon the gorge. Let the tongue,
in its wisdom,
release its stores,

let the mouth, tired of talking, relax into its meant shapes of
give
and receive, its plush

swelling, its slick round reveling, its primal reminiscence
that knows
only the one robust world.

DANCE IN YOUR BLOOD

RUMI

Dance, when you're broken open.
Dance, if you've torn the bandage off.
Dance in the middle of the fighting.
Dance in your blood.
Dance, when you're perfectly free.

TRANSLATED BY COLEMAN BARKS

LATE SELF-PORTRAIT
BY REMBRANDT

Jane Hirshfield

The dog, dead for years, keeps coming back in the dream.
We look at each other there with the old joy.
It was always her gift to bring me into the present—

Which sleeps, changes, awakens, dresses, leaves.

Happiness and unhappiness
differ as a bucket hammered from gold differs from one of
          pressed tin,
this painting proposes.

Each carries the same water, it says.

A BIRTHDAY POEM

TED KOOSER

Just past dawn, the sun stands
with its heavy red head
in a black stanchion of trees,
waiting for someone to come
with his bucket
for the foamy white light,
and then a long day in the pasture.
I too spend my days grazing,
feasting on every green moment
till darkness calls,
and with the others
I walk away into the night,
swinging the little tin bell
of my name.

THE ORGASMS OF ORGANISMS

Dorianne Laux

Above the lawn the wild beetles mate
and mate, skew their tough wings
and join. They light in our hair,
on our arms, fall twirling and twinning
into our laps. And below us, in the grass,
the bugs are seeking each other out,
antennae lifted and trembling, tiny legs
scuttling, then the infinitesimal
ah's of their meeting, the awkward joy
of their turnings around. O end to end
they meet again and swoon as only bugs can.
This is why, sometimes, the grass feels electric
under our feet, each blade quivering, and why
the air comes undone over our heads
and washes down around our ears like rain.
But it has to be spring, and you have to be
in love—acutely, painfully, achingly in love—
to hear the black-robed choir of their sighs.

VARIATION ON A THEME BY RILKE
(*The Book of Hours*, Book I, Poem I, Stanza I)

DENISE LEVERTOV

A certain day became a presence to me;
there it was, confronting me—a sky, air, light:
a being. And before it started to descend
from the height of noon, it leaned over
and struck my shoulder as if with
the flat of a sword, granting me
honor and a task. The day's blow
rang out, metallic—or it was I, a bell awakened,
and what I heard was my whole self
saying and singing what it knew: *I can.*

FULL SUMMER

Sharon Olds

I paused, and paused, over your body,
to feel the current of desire pull
and pull through me. Our hair was still wet,
mine like knotted wrack, it fell
across you as I paused, a soaked coil
around your glans. When one of your hairs
dried, it lifted like a bare nerve.
On the beach, above us, a cloud had appeared in
the clear air, a clockwise loop coming
in out of nothing, now the skin of your scrotum
moved like a live being, an animal,
I began to lick you, the foreskin lightly
stuck in one spot, like a petal, I love
to free it—just so—in joy,
and to sip from the little crying lips
at the tip. Then there was no more pausing,
nor was this the taker,
some new one came
and sucked, and up from where I had been hiding I was

drawn in a heavy spiral out of matter
over into another world
I had thought I would have to die to reach.

POEM IN OCTOBER

DYLAN THOMAS

It was my thirtieth year to heaven
Woke to my hearing from harbour and neighbour wood
   And the mussel pooled and the heron
          Priested shore
          The morning beckon
With water praying and call of seagull and rook
And the knock of sailing boats on the webbed wall
          Myself to set foot
          That second
In the still sleeping town and set forth.

My birthday began with the water—
Birds and the birds of the winged trees flying my name
   Above the farms and the white horses
          And I rose
          In a rainy autumn
And walked abroad in a shower of all my days.
High tide and the heron dived when I took the road
          Over the border
          And the gates
Of the town closed as the town awoke.

A springful of larks in a rolling
Cloud and the roadside bushes brimming with whistling
    Blackbirds and the sun of October
            Summery
        On the hill's shoulder,
Here were fond climates and sweet singers suddenly
Come in the morning where I wandered and listened
        To the rain wringing
            Wind blow cold
    In the wood faraway under me.

    Pale rain over the dwindling harbour
And over the sea wet church the size of a snail
    With its horns through mist and the castle
            Brown as owls
            But all the gardens
Of spring and summer were blooming in the tall tales
Beyond the border and under the lark full cloud.
        There could I marvel
            My birthday
    Away but the weather turned around.

    It turned away from the blithe country
And down the other air and the blue altered sky
    Streamed again a wonder of summer
            With apples

Pears and red currants
And I saw in the turning so clearly a child's
Forgotten mornings when he walked with his mother
  Through the parables
    Of sun light
And the legends of the green chapels

  And the twice told fields of infancy
That his tears burned my cheeks and his heart moved in mine.
  These were the woods the river and sea
        Where a boy
      In the listening
Summertime of the dead whispered the truth of his joy
To the trees and the stones and the fish in the tide.
      And the mystery
        Sang alive
Still in the water and singingbirds.

  And there could I marvel my birthday
Away but the weather turned around. And the true
  Joy of the long dead child sang burning
        In the sun.
      It was my thirtieth
Year to heaven stood there then in the summer noon
Though the town below lay leaved with October blood.
    O may my heart's truth
        Still be sung
  On this high hill in a year's turning.

A THING OF BEAUTY
IS A JOY FOR EVER

JOHN KEATS *(Excerpt)*

A thing of beauty is a joy for ever:
Its loveliness increases; it will never
Pass into nothingness; but still will keep
A bower quiet for us, and a sleep
Full of sweet dreams, and health, and quiet breathing.
Therefore, on every morrow, are we wreathing
A flowery band to bind us to the earth,
Spite of despondence, of the inhuman dearth
Of noble natures, of the gloomy days,
Of all the unhealthy and o'er-darkened ways
Made for our searching: yes, in spite of all,
Some shape of beauty moves away the pall
From our dark spirits. Such the sun, the moon,
Trees old, and young, sprouting a shady boon
For simple sheep; and such are daffodils
With the green world they live in; and clear rills
That for themselves a cooling covert make
'Gainst the hot season; the mid forest brake,
Rich with a sprinkling of fair musk-rose blooms:
And such too is the grandeur of the dooms
We have imagined for the mighty dead;

All lovely tales that we have heard or read:
An endless fountain of immortal drink,
Pouring unto us from the heaven's brink.

Nor do we merely feel these essences
For one short hour; no, even as the trees
That whisper round a temple become soon
Dear as the temple's self, so does the moon,
The passion poesy, glories infinite,
Haunt us till they become a cheering light
Unto our souls, and bound to us so fast
That, whether there be shine or gloom o'ercast,
They always must be with us, or we die.

Therefore, 'tis with full happiness that I
Will trace the story of Endymion.
The very music of the name has gone
Into my being, and each pleasant scene
Is growing fresh before me as the green
Of our own vallies: so I will begin
Now while I cannot hear the city's din;
Now while the early budders are just new,
And run in mazes of the youngest hue
About old forests; while the willow trails
Its delicate amber; and the dairy pails
Bring home increase of milk. And, as the year
Grows lush in juicy stalks, I'll smoothly steer
My little boat, for many quiet hours,
With streams that deepen freshly into bowers.
Many and many a verse I hope to write,

Before the daisies, vermeil rimm'd and white,
Hide in deep herbage; and ere yet the bees
Hum about globes of clover and sweet peas,
I must be near the middle of my story.
O may no wintry season, bare and hoary,
See it half finished: but let Autumn bold,
With universal tinge of sober gold,
Be all about me when I make an end!
And now at once, adventuresome, I send
My herald thought into a wilderness:
There let its trumpet blow, and quickly dress
My uncertain path with green, that I may speed
Easily onward, thorough flowers and weed.

FROM *ENDYMION*, BOOK I

THE SOURCE OF JOY
Rumi

No one knows what makes the soul wake
up so happy! Maybe a dawn breeze has

blown the veil from the face of God.
A thousand new moons appear. Roses

open laughing. Hearts become perfect
rubies like those from Badakshan. The

body turns entirely spirit. Leaves
become branches in this wind. Why is

it now so easy to surrender, even for
those already surrendered? There's no

answer to any of this. No one knows
the source of joy. A poet breathes

into a reed flute, and the tip of
every hair makes music. Shams sails

down clods of dirt from the roof, and
we take jobs as doorkeepers for him.

TRANSLATED BY COLEMAN BARKS

WRITTEN IN A CAREFREE MOOD
Lu Yu

Old man pushing seventy,
in truth he acts like a little boy,
whooping with delight when he spies some mountain fruits,
laughing with joy, tagging after village mummers;
with the others having fun stacking tiles to make a pagoda,
standing alone staring at his image in a jardiniere pool.
Tucked under his arm, a battered book to read,
just like the time he first set off for school.

TRANSLATED BY BURTON WATSON

1192, in Shao-hsing; the mummers of line four are villagers
dressed up in costume who go from house to house at the
beginning of spring, driving out evil spirits.

NEW SHINING WORLDS

Irving Layton

For S. Ross

Solitary
as that lightning-blasted birch
I take comfort from leaves
falling

They tell me nothing
                              endures forever
neither civilizations
nor a woman's malice

Denuding the thicket
leaf by leaf
decay and the punishing minutes
this day
gladden my heart with promise

Only from rot
are new shining worlds begot.

SONNETS TO ORPHEUS: X

RAINER MARIA RILKE

You stone coffins of the ancient world, I think of you
with joy, you who have never left my feelings,
through which the joyful waters of the days
of Rome flow like some walker's singing.

Or those other graves so open, like the eyes
of a shepherd who wakes up glad,
inside full of silence and pale nettles—
excited butterflies came flying out of them—

Now I turn joyfully to everything that has been torn
away from doubt, the mouths open again,
after having known what silence is.

Do we know what silence is, my friends, or not?
This life that faces both ways
has marked the human face from within.

TRANSLATED BY ROBERT BLY

I AM REALLY JUST A TAMBOURINE
Hafiz

Good
Poetry
Makes the universe admit a
Secret:
"I am
Really just a tambourine,
Grab hold,
Play me
Against your warm
Thigh."

TRANSLATED BY DANIEL LADINSKY

A WILD PECULIAR JOY

Irving Layton

King David, flushed with wine,
     is dancing before the Ark;
the virgins are whispering to each other
and the elders are pursing their lips
     but the king knows the Lord delights
in the sight of a valorous man
dancing in the pride of life.

For the Lord of Israel sometimes
     also reels on drunken feet: see,
in the wayward flight of eagles and moths,
in thunderstorms and when lightning
     rives the cedars of Lebanon,
O the Lord wheels in blazing footgear
above the hills of Jerusalem.

King David is circling the Ark
     on reeling feet, and he sings:
"Ho, Israelites, hear me! Hear me, everyone!
God himself staggers on drunken feet

and each night wearing
for raiment the flame of our campfires
He dances in our valleys North and South!"

Black-bearded stalwarts leap up to follow him
    as he stumbles around the Ark;
no one listens, none in the throng is fired
with his wild peculiar joy. So bowing low
    he kisses the Ark thrice
and with a last joyous cry reels singing to his tent
to compose a boisterous hymn in praise of the Lord.

CUTTING LOOSE

William Stafford

For James Dickey

Sometimes from sorrow, for no reason,
you sing. For no reason, you accept
the way of being lost, cutting loose from
all else and electing a world
where you go where you want to.

Arbitrary, sound comes, a reminder
that a steady center is holding
all else. If you listen, that sound
will tell where it is, and you
can slide your way past trouble.

Certain twisted monsters
always bar the path—but that's when
you get going best, glad to be
lost, learning how real it is
here on the earth, again and again.

PLUCKING THE RUSHES

Anonymous *(Chinese, fourth century)*

(A Boy and Girl Are Sent to Gather Rushes for Thatching)

Green rushes with red shoots,
Long leaves bending to the wind—
You and I in the same boat
Plucking rushes at the Five Lakes.
We started at dawn from the orchid-island:
We rested under the elms till noon.
You and I plucking rushes
Had not plucked a handful when night came!

TRANSLATED BY ARTHUR WALEY

ETERNITY

William Blake

He who binds to himself a joy
Does the winged life destroy;
But he who kisses the joy as it flies
Lives in eternity's sun rise.

your little voice
E. E. Cummings

your little voice
        Over the wires came leaping
and i felt suddenly
dizzy
     With the jostling and shouting of merry flowers
wee skipping high-heeled flames
courtesied before my eyes
              or twinkling over to my side
Looked up
with impertinently exquisite faces
floating hands were laid upon me
I was whirled and tossed into delicious dancing
up
Up
with the pale important
         stars and the Humorous
              moon

dear girl
How i was crazy how i cried when i heard
          over time

and tide and death
leaping
Sweetly
your voice

WHEN THE VIOLIN

Hafiz

When
The violin
Can forgive the past

It starts singing.

When the violin can stop worrying
About the future

You will become
Such a drunk laughing nuisance

That God
Will then lean down
And start combing you into
His
Hair.

When the violin can forgive
Every wound caused by
Others

The heart starts
Singing.

Translated by Daniel Ladinsky

VISITATION

Mark Doty

When I heard he had entered the harbor,
and circled the wharf for days,
I expected the worst: shallow water,

confusion, some accident to bring
the young humpback to grief.
Don't they depend on a compass

lodged in the salt-flooded folds
of the brain, some delicate
musical mechanism to navigate

their true course? How many ways,
in our century's late iron hours,
might we have led him to disaster?

That, in those days, was how
I'd come to see the world:
dark upon dark, any sense

of spirit an embattled flame
sparked against wind-driven rain
till pain snuffed it out. I thought,

This is what experience gives us,
and I moved carefully through my life
while I waited. . . . Enough,

it wasn't that way at all. The whale
—exuberant, proud maybe, playful,
like the early music of Beethoven—

cruised the footings for smelts
clustered near the pylons
in mercury flocks. He

(do I have the gender right?)
would negotiate the rusty hulls
of the Portuguese fishing boats

—Holy Infant, Little Marie—
with what could only be read
as pleasure, coming close

then diving, trailing on the surface
big spreading circles
until he'd breach, thrilling us

with the release of pressured breath,
and the bulk of his sleek young head
—a wet black leather sofa

already barnacled with ghostly lice—
and his elegant and unlikely mouth,
and the marvelous afterthought of the flukes,

and the way his broad flippers
resembled a pair of clownish gloves
or puppet hands, looming greenish white

beneath the bay's clouded sheen.
When he had consumed his pleasure
of the shimmering swarm, his pleasure, perhaps,

in his own admired performance,
he swam out the harbor mouth,
into the Atlantic. And though grief

has seemed to me itself a dim,
salt suspension in which I've moved,
blind thing, day by day,

through the wreckage, barely aware
of what I stumbled toward, even I
couldn't help but look

at the way this immense figure
graces the dark medium,
and shines so: heaviness

which is no burden to itself.
What did you think, that joy
was some slight thing?

WHEN I WAS YOUNG

Erica Ehrenberg

When I was young, I had sex
with boys without touching them.
It was very quick and often
happened in English class, like the passing
of an insect through a doorway.
I didn't know what was going on,
but all the windows would open
and it would be raining.
It had nothing to do with hands, no fingers
grazing over notebooks, nothing like that.
Have you ever walked across a plank
inside a defunct factory? And suddenly,
during the tour, some spigot
pops and a wild pressure of different air
sprays into the room, and you don't know
whether or not this is an emergency,
but you can see that at one time
the giant machines pushed and boiled and set off
a motion that became a smoke, or a pile
of dust, and the din was loud, and the day outside
went quiet? One or two times

I got in trouble, but this was for not paying attention.
You see, there was nothing suspect,
not a single wayward hair.

THE WHITE LILIES

LOUISE GLÜCK

As a man and woman make
a garden between them like
a bed of stars, here
they linger in the summer evening
and the evening turns
cold with their terror: it
could all end, it is capable
of devastation. All, all
can be lost, through scented air
the narrow columns
uselessly rising, and beyond,
a churning sea of poppies—

Hush, beloved. It doesn't matter to me
how many summers I live to return:
this one summer we have entered eternity.
I felt your two hands
bury me to release its splendor.

UPON JULIA'S CLOTHES

ROBERT HERRICK

Whenas in silks my Julia goes,
Then, then, methinks, how sweetly flows
That liquefaction of her clothes.

Next, when I cast mine eyes, and see
That brave vibration, each way free,
O, how that glittering taketh me!

i like my body when it is with your body

~ E. E. CUMMINGS

i like my body when it is with your
body.   It is so quite new a thing.
Muscles better and nerves more.
i like your body.   i like what it does,
i like its hows.   i like to feel the spine
of your body and its bones, and the trembling
-firm-smooth ness and which i will
again and again and again
kiss,   i like kissing this and that of you,
i like, slowly stroking the, shocking fuzz
of your electric fur, and what-is-it comes
over parting flesh. . . . And eyes big love-crumbs,

and possibly i like the thrill

of under me you so quite new

IT'S THIS WAY

Nazim Hikmet

I stand in the advancing light,
my hands hungry, the world beautiful.

My eyes can't get enough of the trees—
they're so hopeful, so green.

A sunny road runs through the mulberries,
I'm at the window of the prison infirmary.

I can't smell the medicines—
carnations must be blooming nearby.

It's this way:
being captured is beside the point,
the point is not to surrender.

TRANSLATED BY RANDY BLASING
AND MUTLU KONUK

THE WIDENING SKY

Edward Hirsch

I am so small walking on the beach
at night under the widening sky.
The wet sand quickens beneath my feet
and the waves thunder against the shore.

I am moving away from the boardwalk
with its colorful streamers of people
and the hotels with their blinking lights.
The wind sighs for hundreds of miles.

I am disappearing so far into the dark
I have vanished from sight.
I am a tiny seashell
that has secretly drifted ashore

and carries the sound of the ocean
surging through its body.
I am so small now no one can see me.
How can I be filled with such a vast love?

ONLY WHEN I AM QUIET AND DO NOT SPEAK

Jane Hirshfield

Only when I am quiet for a long time
and do not speak
do the objects of my life draw near.

Shy, the scissors and spoons, the blue mug.
Hesitant even the towels,
for all their intimate knowledge and scent of fresh bleach.

How steady their regard as they ponder,
dreaming and waking,
the entrancement of my daily wanderings and tasks.
Drunk on the honey of feelings, the honey of purpose,
they seem to be thinking,
a quiet judgment that glistens between the glass doorknobs.

Yet theirs is not the false reserve
of a scarcely concealed ill-will,
nor that other, active shying: of pelted rocks.

No, not that. For I hear the sigh of happiness
each object gives off
if I glimpse for even an instant the actual instant—

As if they believed it possible
I might join
their circle of simple, passionate thusness,
their hidden rituals of luck and solitude,
the joyous gap in them where appears in us the pronoun *I*.

PIED BEAUTY

Gerard Manley Hopkins

Glory be to God for dappled things—
   For skies of couple-colour as a brinded cow;
     For rose-moles all in stipple upon trout that swim;
Fresh-firecoal chestnut-falls; finches' wings;
   Landscape plotted and pieced—fold, fallow, and plough;
     And áll trádes, their gear and tackle and trim.

All things counter, original, spare, strange;
   Whatever is fickle, freckled (who knows how?)
     With swift, slow; sweet, sour; adazzle, dim;
He fathers-forth whose beauty is past change:
         Praise him.

I WANT SOMETHING WITHOUT A NAME

Erica Ehrenberg

I want something without a name—No!
I'm not saying I don't know what I crave!
I want something without a name, light of foot, even
airborne, all feathers but feathers
detached in the air,
of fine plumage. I want that which
it will not be possible to say
I have had. What envelops and releases—
not chronologically, but envelops and releases
all at the same time.
One gesture, small as a man's. Passing through a liquid
and a solid state, and then an airborne
state, *not* chronologically, but *all at the same time.*
A brightness in the eye without the eye. No eyes,
no ears, no parts, all opening and closing
at the same time. Both closed and open of no
apparent distance from me. No distance. A hole
with nothing around it. No surroundings. A dive
to and from
not even a pool,
not even a plank.

EVEN IF I DON'T SEE IT AGAIN
Marie Howe

Even if I don't see it again.——nor ever feel it
I know it is——and that if once it hailed me
it ever does——

and so it is myself I want to turn in that direction
not as towards a place, but it was a tilting
within myself,

as one turns a mirror to flash the light to where
it isn't.——I was blinded like that——and swam
in what shone at me

only able to endure it by being no one and so
specifically myself I thought I'd die
from being loved like that.

SITTING UP WITH MY WIFE ON NEW YEAR'S EVE

Hsü Chün-Ch'ien

So many delights the excitement has no end,
so much joy the cup is never still:
pluck a daddy longlegs out of the wine,
find a wild plum inside the dumpling!
The blinds swing open and wind lifts the curtain;
the candle burns low, its wick turned to ash.
No wonder the pins weigh heavy in your hair—
we've waited up so long for dawn light to come!

Translated by Burton Watson

It was the custom at New Year's to place a daddy longlegs,
whose name, *hsi-tzu,* is a homophone for "happiness,"
in the wind, and to hide wild plums in the dumplings.

COW WORSHIP

GERALD STERN

I love the cows best when they are a few feet away
from my dining-room window and my pine floor,
when they reach in to kiss me with their wet
mouths and their white noses.
I love them when they walk over the garbage cans
and across the cellar doors,
over the sidewalk and through the metal chairs
and the birdseed.
—Let me reach out through the thin curtains
and feel the warm air of May.
It is the temperature of the whole galaxy,
all the bright clouds and clusters,
beasts and heroes,
glittering singers and isolated thinkers
at pasture.

BLACKBERRY EATING

Galway Kinnell

I love to go out in late September
among the fat, overripe, icy, black blackberries
to eat blackberries for breakfast,
the stalks very prickly, a penalty
they earn for knowing the black art
of blackberry making; and as I stand among them
lifting the stalks to my mouth, the ripest berries
fall almost unbidden to my tongue,
as words sometimes do, certain peculiar words
like *strengths* or *squinched*, or *broughamed*,
many-lettered, one-syllabled lumps,
which I squeeze, squinch open, and splurge well
in the silent, startled, icy, black language
of blackberry eating in late September.

THE ROUND

Stanley Kunitz

Light splashed this morning
on the shell-pink anemones
swaying on their tall stems;
down blue-spiked veronica
light flowed in rivulets
over the humps of the honeybees;
this morning I saw light kiss
the silk of the roses
in their second flowering,
my late bloomers
flushed with their brandy.
A curious gladness shook me.

So I have shut the doors of my house,
so I have trudged downstairs to my cell,
so I am sitting in semi-dark
hunched over my desk
with nothing for a view
to tempt me
but a bloated compost heap,
steamy old stinkpile,

under my window;
and I pick my notebook up
and I start to read aloud
the still-wet words I scribbled
on the blotted page:
"Light splashed . . ."

I can scarcely wait till tomorrow
when a new life begins for me,
as it does each day,
as it does each day.

A SUMMER DAY
Li Po

Naked I lie in the green forest of summer. . . .
Too lazy to wave my white feathered fan.
I hang my cap on a crag,
And bare my head to the wind that comes
Blowing through the pine trees.

Translated by Shigeyoshi Obata

FIRST THANKSGIVING

Sharon Olds

When she comes back, from college, I will see
the skin of her upper arms, cool,
matte, glossy. She will hug me, my old
soupy chest against her breasts,
I will smell her hair! She will sleep in this apartment,
her sleep like an untamed, good object, like a
soul in a body. She came into my life the
second great arrival, fresh
from the other world—which lay, from within him,
within me. Those nights, I fed her to sleep,
week after week, the moon rising,
and setting, and waxing—whirling, over the months,
in a steady blur, around our planet.
Now she doesn't need love like that, she has
had it. She will walk in glowing, we will talk,
and then, when she's fast asleep, I'll exult
to have her in that room again,
behind that door! As a child, I caught
bees, by the wings, and held them, some seconds,
looked into their wild faces,
listened to them sing, then tossed them back

into the air—I remember the moment the
arc of my toss swerved, and they entered
the corrected curve of their departure.

HERE

GRACE PALEY

Here I am in the garden laughing
an old woman with heavy breasts
and a nicely mapped face

how did this happen
well that's who I wanted to be

at last   a woman
in the old style   sitting
stout thighs apart under
a big skirt   grandchild sliding
on   off my lap   a pleasant
summer perspiration

that's my old man across the yard
he's talking to the meter reader
he's telling him the world's sad story
how electricity is oil or uranium
and so forth   I tell my grandson
run over to your grandpa   ask him

to sit beside me for a minute   I
am suddenly exhausted by my desire
to kiss his sweet explaining lips.

THE PLEASURES OF THE DOOR
Francis Ponge

Kings never touch doors.

They're not familiar with this happiness: to push, gently or roughly before you one of these great, friendly panels, to turn towards it to put it back in place—to hold a door in your arms.

The happiness of seizing one of these tall barriers to a room by the porcelain knob of its belly; this quick hand-to-hand, during which your progress slows for a moment, your eye opens up and your whole body adapts to its new apartment.

With a friendly hand you hold on a bit longer, before firmly pushing it back and shutting yourself in—of which you are agreeably assured by the click of the powerful, well-oiled latch.

TRANSLATED BY C. K. WILLIAMS

GRAPEFRUIT

GERALD STERN

I'm eating breakfast even if it means standing
in front of the sink and tearing at the grapefruit,
even if I'm leaning over to keep the juices
away from my chest and stomach and even if a spider
is hanging from my ear and a wild flea
is crawling down my leg. My window is wavy
and dirty. There is a wavy tree outside
with pitiful leaves in front of the rusty fence
and there is a patch of useless rhubarb, the leaves
bent over, the stalks too large and bitter for eating,
and there is some lettuce and spinach too old for picking
beside the rhubarb. This is the way the saints
ate, only they dug for thistles, the feel
of thorns in the throat it was a blessing, my pity
it knows no bounds. There is a thin tomato plant
inside a rolled-up piece of wire, the worms
are already there, the birds are bored. In time
I'll stand beside the rolled-up fence with tears
of gratitude in my eyes. I'll hold a puny
pinched tomato in my open hand,
I'll hold it to my lips. Blessed art Thou,

King of tomatoes, King of grapefruit. The thistle
must have juices, there must be a trick. I hate
to say it but I'm thinking if there is a saint
in our time what will he be, and what will he eat?
I hated rhubarb, all that stringy sweetness—
a fake applesauce—I hated spinach,
always with egg and vinegar, I hated
oranges when they were quartered, that was the signal
for castor oil—aside from the peeled navel
I love the Florida cut in two. I bend
my head forward, my chin is in the air,
I hold my right hand off to the side, the pinkie
is waving; I am back again at the sink;
oh loneliness, I stand at the sink, my garden
is dry and blooming, I love my lettuce, I love
my cornflowers, the sun is doing it all,
the sun and a little dirt and a little water.
I lie on the ground out there, there is one yard
between the house and the tree; I am more calm there
looking back at this window, looking up
a little at the sky, a blue passageway
with smears of white—and gray—a bird crossing
from berm to berm, from ditch to ditch, another one,
a wild highway, a wild skyway, a flock
of little ones to make me feel gay, they fly
down the thruway, I move my eyes back and forth

to see them appear and disappear, I stretch
my neck, a kind of exercise. Ah sky,
my breakfast is over, my lunch is over, the wind
has stopped, it is the hour of deepest thought.
Now I brood, I grimace, how quickly the day goes,
how full it is of sunshine, and wind, how many
smells there are, how gorgeous is the distant
sound of dogs, and engines—Blessed art Thou
Lord of the falling leaf, Lord of the rhubarb,
Lord of the roving cat, Lord of the cloud.
Blessed art Thou oh grapefruit King of the universe,
Blessed art Thou my sink, oh Blessed art Thou
Thou milkweed Queen of the sky, burster of seeds,
Who bringeth forth juice from the earth.

IN PRAISE OF DREAMS

Wislawa Szymborska

In my dreams
I paint like Vermeer van Delft.

I speak fluent Greek
and not just with the living.

I drive a car
that does what I want it to.

I am gifted
and write mighty epics.

I hear voices
as clearly as any venerable saint.

My brilliance as a pianist
would stun you.

I fly the way we ought to,
i.e., on my own.

Falling from the roof,
I tumble gently to the grass.

I've got no problem
breathing under water.

I can't complain:
I've been able to locate Atlantis.

It's gratifying that I can always
wake up before dying.

As soon as war breaks out,
I roll over on my other side.

I'm a child of my age,
but I don't have to be.

A few years ago
I saw two suns.

And the night before last a penguin,
clear as day.

TRANSLATED BY STANISLAW BARAŃCZAK
AND CLARE CAVANAGH

ALLEGRO

Tomas Tranströmer

After a black day, I play Haydn,
and feel a little warmth in my hands.

The keys are ready. Kind hammers fall.
The sound is spirited, green, and full of silence.

The sound says that freedom exists
and someone pays no taxes to Caesar.

I shove my hands in my haydnpockets
and act like a man who is calm about it all.

I raise my haydnflag. The signal is:
"We do not surrender. But want peace."

The music is a house of glass standing on a slope;
rocks are flying, rocks are rolling.

The rocks roll straight through the house
but every pane of glass is still whole.

TRANSLATED BY ROBERT BLY

THE GREAT SEA

Uvavnuk

The great sea
frees me, moves me,
as a strong river carries a weed.
Earth and her strong winds
move me, take me away,
and my soul is swept up in joy.

TRANSLATED BY JANE HIRSHFIELD

THIS IS JUST TO SAY

William Carlos Williams

I have eaten
the plums
that were in
the icebox

and which
you were probably
saving
for breakfast

Forgive me
they were delicious
so sweet
and so cold

A BLESSING

James Wright

Just off the highway to Rochester, Minnesota,
Twilight bounds softly forth on the grass.
And the eyes of those two Indian ponies
Darken with kindness.
They have come gladly out of the willows
To welcome my friend and me.
We step over the barbed wire into the pasture
Where they have been grazing all day, alone.
They ripple tensely, they can hardly contain their happiness
That we have come.
They bow shyly as wet swans. They love each other.
There is no loneliness like theirs.
At home once more,
They begin munching the young tufts of spring in
      the darkness.
I would like to hold the slenderer one in my arms,
For she has walked over to me
And nuzzled my left hand.
She is black and white,
Her mane falls wild on her forehead,
And the light breeze moves me to caress her long ear

That is delicate as the skin over a girl's wrist.
Suddenly I realize
That if I stepped out of my body I would break
Into blossom.

THE LAKE ISLE OF INNISFREE

W. B. YEATS

I will arise and go now, and go to Innisfree,
And a small cabin build there, of clay and wattles made:
Nine bean-rows will I have there, a hive for the honey-bee,
And live alone in the bee-loud glade.

And I shall have some peace there, for peace comes
  dropping slow,
Dropping from the veils of the morning to where the
  cricket sings;
There midnight's all a glimmer, and noon a purple glow,
And evening full of the linnet's wings.

I will arise and go now, for always night and day
I hear lake water lapping with low sounds by the shore;
While I stand on the roadway, or on the pavements grey,
I hear it in the deep heart's core.

MATINS

Denise Levertov *(Excerpt)*

ii

The authentic! I said
rising from the toilet seat.
The radiator in rhythmic knockings
spoke of the rising steam.
The authentic, I said
breaking the handle of my hairbrush as I
brushed my hair in
rhythmic strokes: That's it,
that's joy, it's always
a recognition, the known
appearing fully itself, and
more itself than one knew.

vii

Marvelous Truth, confront us
at every turn,
in every guise, iron ball,
egg, dark horse, shadow,
cloud
of breath on the air,

dwell
in our crowded hearts
our steaming bathrooms, kitchens full of
things to be done, the
ordinary streets.
Thrust close your smile
that we know you, terrible joy.

I COME HOME WANTING TO TOUCH EVERYONE

STEPHEN DUNN

The dogs greet me, I descend
into their world of fur and tongues
and then my wife and I embrace
as if we'd just closed the door
in a motel, our two girls slip in
between us and we're all saying
each other's names and the dogs
Buster and Sundown are on their hind legs,
people-style, seeking more love.
I've come home wanting to touch
everyone, everything; usually I turn
the key and they're all lost
in food or homework, even the dogs
are preoccupied with themselves,
I desire only to ease
back in, the mail, a drink,
but tonight the body-hungers have sent out
their long-range signals
or love itself has risen
from its squalor of neglect.
Everytime the kids turn their backs

I touch my wife's breasts
and when she checks the dinner
the unfriendly cat on the dishwasher
wants to rub heads, starts to speak
with his little motor and violin—
everything, everyone is intelligible
in the language of touch,
and we sit down to dinner inarticulate
as blood, all difficulties postponed
because the weather is so good.

SNOW GEESE

Mary Oliver

Oh, to love what is lovely, and will not last!
    What a task
      to ask

of anything, or anyone,

yet it is ours,
  and not by the century or the year, but by the hours.

One fall day I heard
  above me, and above the sting of the wind, a sound
I did not know, and my look shot upward; it was

a flock of snow geese, winging it
  faster than the ones we usually see,
and, being the color of snow, catching the sun

so they were, in part at least, golden. I

held my breath
as we do

sometimes
to stop time
when something wonderful
has touched us

as with a match
which is lit, and bright,
but does not hurt
in the common way,
but delightfully,
as if delight
were the most serious thing
you ever felt.

The geese
flew on.
I have never
seen them again.

Maybe I will, someday, somewhere.
Maybe I won't.
It doesn't matter.
What matters
is that, when I saw them,
I saw them
as through the veil, secretly, joyfully, clearly.

WHY

WENDELL BERRY

Why all the embarrassment
about being happy?
Sometimes I'm as happy
as a sleeping dog,
and for the same reasons,
and for others.

About the Poets

KIM ADDONIZIO (b. 1954) has published four poetry collections, most recently *What Is This Thing Called Love* in 2005. Her first novel, *Little Beauties,* was also published in 2005. She lives and teaches creative writing in San Francisco. A poem by her appears on page 35.

ANNA AKHMATOVA (1889–1966). The young Akhmatova knew French as well as the Russian poets by heart. Her first poetry collection, *Evening,* appeared in 1912. Three marriages and several more collections followed, though after 1922 she had nothing else published because her apolitical work was considered incompatible with the new order. Toward the end of her life, however, the ailing Akhmatova was acknowledged as the grande dame of Russian literature. A poem by her appears on page 63.

PETRONIUS ARBITER (c. 27–c. 66) was a poet and writer in the Roman Empire, though nothing is known of his exact dates or where he lived. His sole surviving complete work is a racy tale called *Satyricon.* A poem by him appears on page 30.

WENDELL BERRY (b. 1934), a farmer, lives in his native Kentucky. He is the author of more than thirty books of poetry, essays, and novels. His latest collection of poetry is *Given.* Poems by him appear on pages 49, 51, and 175.

WILLIAM BLAKE (1757–1827) was an English poet, painter, visionary, mystic, and engraver. Blake proclaimed the supremacy of the imagination over the rationalism and materialism of eighteenth-century England. His first book of poems, *Poetical Works,* was published in 1778, followed by *Songs of Innocence* in 1789 and *Songs of Experience* in 1794. His most famous poem, "The Tyger," is in *Songs of Experience.* Dismissed as an eccentric in his time,

Blake today is highly regarded both as an artist and a poet. A poem by him appears on page 126.

ROBERT BLY (b. 1926), poet, editor, translator, storyteller, and father of what he has called the "expressive men's movement," was born in Minnesota to parents of Norwegian stock. In 1956 he went to Norway on a Fulbright scholarship to translate Norwegian poetry into English. He returned to start a literary review, *The 50's,* then *The 60's* and *The 70's,* which introduced these poets to his generation. During the seventies, he had eleven books of poetry, essays, and translations published, with four more appearing in the eighties. His most recent collection is *My Sentence Is a Thousand Years of Joy* (2005). A poem by him appears on page 66.

HAYDEN CARRUTH (b. 1921) was born in Connecticut and was educated at the University of North Carolina and the University of Chicago. He has spent much of his life in northern Vermont, though he now lives in upstate New York, where until recently he taught in the graduate creative writing program at Syracuse University. He has published twenty-nine books, mostly poetry, but also four books of criticism and two anthologies. His collection *Scrambled Eggs and Whiskey* won the National Book Award for Poetry. He has also won the National Book Critics Circle Award, the Lannan Award, and many other honors. A poem by him appears on page 31.

RAYMOND CARVER (1938–1988) was a major force in the revitalization of the American short story in the eighties and is better known for his stories than his poetry. His poetry was in the vernacular, lyric-narrative style of William Carlos Williams. His father, a sawmill worker in Oregon, was an alcoholic. Carver received his BA from Humboldt College, California, in 1963. He later went on to teach at the Iowa Writer's Workshop in 1973 with John Cheever, though he said later that they did nothing but drink. Carver died an alcoholic at the age of fifty. A poem by him appears on page 93.

LUCILLE CLIFTON (b. 1936) came from a working-class family in upstate New York. Her parents, though not formally educated, provided their large family with an appreciation and an abundance of books, especially those by African Americans. Clifton was a drama major at Howard University in Washington, D.C., and after leaving university she began to cultivate in poetry the minimalist characteristics that would become her professional signature. Like other black aesthetic poets, she broke with Eurocentric conventions and developed untitled free-verse lyrics with sparse punctuation. Her most recent collection is *Blessing the Boats: 1988–2000*. A poem by her appears on page 39.

BILLY COLLINS (b. 1941) is professor of English at Lehman College, the City University of New York. He lives in Somers, New York. No poet since Robert Frost has managed to combine high critical acclaim with such popular appeal. The typical Collins poem opens on a clear and hospitable note but soon takes an unexpected turn. Poems that begin in irony may end in a moment of lyrical surprise. No wonder Collins sees his poetry as "a form of travel writing" and considers humor "a door into the serious." The author of several volumes of poetry, Collins was poet laureate of the United States from 2001 to 2003. Poems by him appear on pages 40, 58, and 84.

E. E. CUMMINGS (1894–1962) was born in Cambridge, Massachusetts. In his poetry he experimented radically with form, punctuation, spelling, and syntax, creating a new, highly personal means of poetic expression. At the time of his death, he was the second most widely read poet in the United States, after Robert Frost. Poems by him appear on pages 127 and 139.

DANTE ALIGHIERI (1265–1321), a native of Florence, fell in love while still a youth with a girl named Bice di Folco Portinari, whom he subsequently referred to in his works as Beatrice, the muse of his entire lifetime. Beatrice died quite young, though Dante married Gemma Donati, with whom he had three children, while Beatrice was still alive. He entered Florentine politics and allied himself with a party that fell from grace, which resulted in his being exiled from his native city for the rest of his life. He never returned and was given refuge in various Italian cities, eventually dying in

Ravenna; not, however, before writing his masterpiece *The Divine Comedy,* one of the greatest achievements in all European literature. A poem by him appears on page 90.

EMILY DICKINSON (1830–1886) was an obsessively private writer, with only seven of her some eighteen hundred poems being published during her lifetime. She withdrew from social contact at the age of twenty-three, took to wearing only white, and devoted herself to writing in secret. She was born in Amherst, Massachusetts, to a family well known for its political and educational activity. After beginning in a conventional style, she began experimenting, and her frequent use of dashes, off-rhymes, broken meter, and unconventional metaphors has since given her the reputation of being one of the most innovative poets of the nineteenth century. Her sister Lavinia first brought out Emily's poems after her death. Poems by her appear on pages 83 and 87.

MARK DOTY (b. 1953) is the author of several collections of poetry, including *School of the Arts* (2005). He has received numerous fellowships and prizes, including Britain's T. S. Eliot Prize. He has also written *Firebird,* an autobiography, and *Heaven's Coast: A Memoir.* He teaches at the University of Houston. A poem by him appears on page 131.

STEPHEN DUNN (b. 1939) is professor of creative writing at Richard Stockton College of New Jersey. He has published over a dozen collections of poetry, including *Different Hours,* for which he won the Pulitzer Prize in 2000, and, most recently, *The Insistence of Beauty* (2005). His poetry draws from considered reflection on individual experience. It asks important questions about what it means to be an American, to be a man, and to be a poet alive and imagining his way into the twenty-first century. Poems by him appear on pages 27 and 171.

ERICA EHRENBERG (b. 1978) lives in New York City. She is a graduate of Amherst College and of the creative writing MFA program at New York University. Her poems have appeared in various magazines and journals, including the *New Republic*, the *Saint Ann's Review*, *Good Foot, jubilat*, and www.unpleasanteventschedule.com. Poems by her appear on pages 135 and 145.

ANNE FINCH (1661–1720), maid of honor to Mary of Modena at the Stuart court of James II, married Colonel Finch and, through that marriage, eventually became Countess of Winchilsea. Highly educated, Anne was one of the earliest published women poets in England, considered by some to be the finest prior to the nineteenth century. She received the active support and encouragement of not only her husband, but also of Jonathan Swift and Alexander Pope. The recognized collection of her work is *The Poems of Anne, Countess of Winchilsea*, edited by Myra Reynolds in 1903. A poem by her appears on page 79.

JACK GILBERT (b. 1925). Soon after the publication of his first collection, *Views of Jeopardy*, which was nominated for a Pulitzer Prize, Gilbert moved to Europe on a Guggenheim Fellowship and disappeared from the American literary world for twenty years to live a simple, anonymous life on a remote Greek island. He later returned to the United States, held various teaching jobs, and was the recipient of several awards. His fourth collection, *Refusing Heaven*, was published in 2005. His poems have appeared in the *New Yorker* and in all the major poetry magazines. He now lives in western Massachusetts. A poem by him appears on page 23.

LOUISE GLÜCK (b. 1943) commonly addresses the themes of loss, rejection, and isolation in her work, though frequently these are transformed through the creation of art. She is the author of numerous books of poetry and has won the Pulitzer Prize (*The Wild Iris*) and the National Book Critics Circle Award (*Triumph of Achilles*) as well as many other awards and fellowships. In 2003 she assumed her duties as the Library of Congress's twelfth Poet Laureate Consultant in Poetry. A poem by her appears on page 137.

HAFIZ (c. 1317–1389) is widely recognized as the preeminent master of the Persian ghazal form. In the tradition of Rumi, he is one of the great Sufi poets, and in Iran, his principal work, the *Divan,* is revered almost as much as the Qur'an. Well educated, fluent in both Persian and Arabic, Hafiz memorized the Qur'an at an early age. He was born in Shiraz and is buried there in the Musalla Gardens, on the banks of the river. Poems by him appear on pages 45, 121, and 129.

HAN SHAN (ninth century) means "Cold Mountain," the pseudonym this Chinese poet and recluse hid his true identity behind. There are two distinct biographical traditions about him. The first emphasizes his eccentricity, his visits to a Buddhist temple to do odd jobs, or to poke fun at the monks' self-importance. The second is based on the biographical elements found in his three-hundred-plus poems. Han Shan was born to privilege, married, and had a son. In a local rebellion against the emperor, Han Shan fled for his life with his family to the Tientai Mountains and forged a new identity as a hermit. The poems reveal a thorough knowledge of Confucian, Taoist, and Buddhist sources, as well as of poetry and literature. He never professed a particular creed, but freely borrowed from all traditions. A poem by him appears on page 78.

ROBERT HERRICK (1591–1674) was born in London, the son of a prosperous goldsmith. In 1613 he went to St. John's College, Cambridge, and became the eldest of the Cavalier Poets, a group of young men who idolized Ben Jonson. In 1623 he became an Anglican minister and was sent to a country diocese where he wrote some of his best work. *Hesperides,* his major collection of twelve hundred poems, was published in 1648. He died a bachelor at the age of eighty-three. A poem by him appears on page 138.

NAZIM HIKMET (1902–1963) was one of the most important figures in twentieth-century Turkish literature and was one of the first to use more or less free verse. His work was translated into several languages, and in his lifetime he was the best-known Turkish poet in the West. In Turkey he was condemned for his commitment to Marxism and for his social criticism. He was the only major writer to speak out against the Armenian massacres in 1915 and 1922. He spent seventeen years in prison and called poetry "the bloodiest of the arts." He was finally released in 1950 because of international protests and lived the rest of his life in Warsaw and Moscow. A poem by him appears on page 140.

EDWARD HIRSCH (b. 1950) received his PhD in folklore from the University of Pennsylvania. He is the author of several books of poetry, including *Wild Gratitude,* which won the National Book Critics Circle Award in 1986, and he is the recipient of many other awards and fellowships. He is currently president of John Simon Guggenheim Memorial Foundation. A poem by him appears on page 141.

JANE HIRSHFIELD (b. 1953) is a prize-winning poet, translator, editor, and author of six collections of poetry. Her work addresses the life of the passions, the way the objects and events of everyday life are informed by deeper wisdoms and by the darkness and losses of life. Her poetry continually searches for the point where new knowledge of the world and self may appear and carries the influence of her lifelong study and practice of Buddhism. Originally from New York City, she has lived in the Bay Area for many years. Poems by her appear on pages 98, 104, and 142.

TONY HOAGLAND (b. 1954) teaches in the graduate writing program at the University of Houston. He is the author of three collections of poetry, including *What Narcissism Means to Me* (2003). His acute irony explores the hidden layers of not only his own personal life, but also of American culture in general, and his work is characterized by humor and moral intelligence. In 2005 he was awarded the Mark Twain Poetry Award, which recognizes a poet's contribution to humor in American poetry. A poem by him appears on page 28.

GERARD MANLEY HOPKINS (1844–1889) was educated at Oxford University, entered the Catholic Church in 1866, and was ordained a Jesuit priest in 1877. On becoming Catholic, he burned much of his early verse and abandoned the writing of poetry. Then, in 1875, the sinking of a German ship inspired him to write one of his most impressive poems, "The Wreck of the Deutschland," and he went on to produce his greatest work in the later years of his life. A poem by him appears on page 144.

MARIE HOWE (b. 1950) has published poems in the *New Yorker,* the *Atlantic, Harvard Review,* and *New England Review,* among others. She is the author of two collections of poetry, the most recent of which, *What the Living Do* (1998), is a result of her self-questioning and grief following the death of her brother from AIDS. Hers is a poetry of intimacy, witness, honesty, and relation. She teaches at Sarah Lawrence College. A poem by her appears on page 146.

HSÜ CHÜN-CH'IEN was a Chinese poet writing in the sixth century. That is all that is known of him. A poem by him appears on page 147.

HOLLY HUGHES (b. 1955) has spent twenty-six summers working on boats in Alaska, both as a deckhand/cook and as a skipper. She spends the winters in Washington, where she teaches writing classes at Edmonds Community College. A finalist for the Arts and Letters Prize in 2003, her poems have appeared in many magazines and journals. She lives in a log cabin built in the thirties in Indianola, Washington. A poem by her appears on page 88.

KABIR (1398–1448?), the son of a weaver, was born in and lived in the holy Hindu city of Banaras. A powerful spiritual teacher, he crossed the sectarian and religious divides of his day to attract both followers and enemies among Muslims and Hindus alike. He is widely thought to have been illiterate, and his poems, which were part of his teaching method, were given orally and written down by others. His central message was the necessity of seeing through our self-deceit to the truth of who we are. To this day, his collected sayings and poems, *The Bijak of Kabir,* is still the scripture of the Kabir

Panth, the monastic order that grew up around Kabir's teachings. A poem by him appears on page 46.

JOHN KEATS (1795–1821) was the last of the great English Romantic poets. When Keats was born, William Blake was almost forty, Wordsworth and Coleridge were in their midtwenties, Byron was a boy of seven, and Shelley was just three. Keats was the most humbly born of them all, his father having run the Swan and Hoop livery stables in central London. Keats's first work, *Poems,* was published in 1817, when he was just twenty-two. In the following three years, he produced his entire output in an astonishing outpouring of creative genius. Next to Wordsworth, Keats is the foremost representative of the Romantic revival of interest in nature. He also held that the imagination was the most important organ of perception. A poem by him appears on page 113.

JANE KENYON (1947–1995) was born in Ann Arbor, Michigan, and received an MA from the University of Michigan in 1972. That same year, she married the poet Donald Hall and moved with him to New Hampshire. She published four books of poetry during her lifetime and a book of translations, *Twenty Poems* by Anna Akhmatova. She died of leukemia in 1995 while poet laureate of New Hampshire. Several more of her works were published posthumously. A poem by her appears on page 52.

GALWAY KINNELL (b. 1927) received the Pulitzer Prize in 1983 for his *Selected Poems.* He has been poet in residence at several universities, as well as a field worker for the Congress of Racial Equality. Robert Langbaum said in the *American Poetry Review* that "Kinnell, at a time when so many poets are content to be skillful and trivial, speaks with a big voice about the whole of life." Throughout his work, he explores his relationship to transience, to death, to the power of wilderness and wildness, and to the primitive underpinnings of existence. He once said that "if you could keep going deeper, you would finally not be a person. . . . You'd be a blade of grass or ultimately, perhaps, a stone. And if a stone could read, poetry would speak for it." A poem by him appears on page 149.

TED KOOSER (b. 1939) is the author of eleven poetry collections and a number of nonfiction works. He has received numerous awards, most recently the Pulitzer Prize for his 2004 collection, *Delights and Shadows*. Known as a writer of place—the Midwest—and for his ability to find the extraordinary in the ordinary, he was appointed the Library of Congress's thirteenth Poet Laureate Consultant in Poetry in 2004. For thirty-five years, he worked for life-insurance companies as an underwriter and an executive. He would write poems before dawn, before leaving for the office. He lives in Nebraska with his wife, Kathleen Rutledge, the editor of the Lincoln *Journal Star*. A poem by him appears on page 105.

STANLEY KUNITZ (1905–2006) worked for many years as an editor in New York City before achieving major recognition for his poetry, which came with a Pulitzer Prize in 1958 for his *Collected Poems*. He went on to win many prizes and honors. In 2000 he was the U.S. poet laureate, and in 1995 his collection *Passing Through* won the National Book Award. He taught for many years in the graduate writing program at Columbia. At age one hundred, he was America's oldest active poet. A poem by him appears on page 150.

DORIANNE LAUX (b. 1952) has an Irish, French, and Algonquin heritage, and she grew up in Maine. Between the ages of eighteen and thirty, she worked as a gas station manager, sanatorium cook, maid, and doughnut-holer. A single mother, she took occasional poetry classes at a local junior college, writing poems during shift breaks. In 1983 she moved to Berkeley and began writing in earnest. Supported by scholarships and grants, she returned to school and graduated in 1988 with a degree in English. She has won various awards and has published three collections of poetry. In the *Gettysburg Review*, Tony Hoagland writes that "Laux is a believer in desire, and she takes her stance as a hero of the ordinary, with both feet planted firmly in the luminous material world." Poems by her appear on pages 100 and 106.

IRVING LAYTON (1912–2006) was born in Romania of Jewish parents who emigrated to Montreal in 1913. Layton was always the nonconformist, and his life went through many changes until he wrote his first major poem in 1946 and saw his destiny materializing. For much of his life he supported his art with teaching, one of his students being Leonard Cohen. He went on to become Canada's most celebrated poet, winning many awards and fellowships, with a large international reputation. He was nominated for the Nobel Prize during the eighties. He had five wives and five children. Poems by him appear on pages 119 and 122.

LI-YOUNG LEE (b. 1957) was born in Jakarta, Indonesia, to Chinese parents. In 1959, the family fled the country to escape anti-Chinese sentiment and eventually settled in the United States in 1964. Lee has published two collections of poetry, has received a number of awards and scholarships, and has taught at several universities. He now lives in Chicago with his wife and two sons. A poem by him appears on page 37.

DENISE LEVERTOV (1923–1997) published her first book, *The Double Image,* which she wrote between the ages of seventeen and twenty-one, in 1946. Soon after emigrating from England to the United States, she was recognized as an important voice in the American avant-garde. Her next book, *With Eyes in the Back of Our Heads,* established her as one of the great American poets, and her English origins were forgotten. She published more than twenty volumes of poetry and taught at Stanford University from 1989 to 1993. She was always an outsider—in England, in America, and in poetry circles—for she never considered herself part of any school. Poems by her appear on pages 107 and 169.

C. S. LEWIS (1898–1963) was an Irish author and scholar from Belfast who lived most of his life in England. He taught at Oxford for thirty years and was later professor of medieval and Renaissance literature at Cambridge. Alongside his scholarly published work, he gained an international reputation for his popular novels for children (the Narnia series), his science fiction, and his Christian novels and apologetics, which included *The Screwtape Letters*. He also wrote three volumes of poetry. He was married for a short time to the American writer Joy Gresham, who died of bone cancer soon after their marriage. A poem by him appears on page 75.

LI PO (701–762) was probably the greatest Chinese poet of premodern times. He brought an unparalleled grace and eloquence to his treatment of traditional themes and a grandeur that lifts his work far above any mere imitation of the past. He grew up in Szechuan, in western China, and later traveled extensively. Around 742, the emperor appointed him to a post in the Hanlin Academy, but a few years later he was exiled from the capital as a result of slanders against him. He later received another position at court but was again exiled and spent the rest of his life as a wanderer. A poem by him appears on page 152.

LU YU (733–804) was an abandoned child in a time of war. Adopted at the age of three by the abbot of Dragon Cloud Buddhist Monastery, he was given the name of Lu Yu. Not wanting to become a monk, he escaped from the monastery when he was thirteen and worked for years as a clown for a group of traveling artists. In 760 he settled in the mountains to investigate the growing of tea. After twenty years of research, he produced *Classic of Tea,* the definitive work on cultivating, making, and drinking tea. Since then, he has been known as the Sage of Tea. A poem by him appears on page 118.

JOHN MASEFIELD (1878–1967) went to sea as a youth and later spent several years in the United States. In 1897 he returned to England and joined the staff of the *Manchester Guardian.* His first two volumes of poetry, *Salt-Water Ballads* and *Ballads,* earned him the title "Poet of the Sea." He was, in fact, a poet, novelist, dramatist, and journalist and was known for a range that encompassed ballads, nature poetry, and mythological narrative. He was the British poet laureate from 1930 until his death. A poem by him appears on page 74.

MARGARET MENGES (b. 1951) lives in Elmira, New York, the town she grew up in in a family of four sisters. She teaches middle-school students and has two sons, David and Daniel. A poem by her appears on page 65.

JOHN MILTON (1608–1674), born in London and one of the greatest poets of the English language, is best known for his great epic poem, *Paradise Lost* (1667). Milton's powerful rhetoric prose and eloquent poetry had an immense influence on eighteenth-century verse. Besides poetry, Milton published pamphlets defending civil and religious rights, including the right to divorce. His first teacher was his father, who instilled in him a love of art and literature. He began writing poetry while at Christ's College, Cambridge, and then continued for several years while living at home with his parents. The Civil Wars silenced his public voice for twenty years, though Milton, a Puritan, continued to work on his great epic and on his studies of Greek, Latin, and Italian. In 1651 he became blind, which served only to deepen his verbal richness. A poem by him appears on page 47.

PABLO NERUDA (1904–1973) is widely considered the most important Latin-American poet of the twentieth century, as well as an influential contributor to major developments in modern poetry. He was born in provincial Chile, the son of a teacher and a railroad worker. He moved to the capital, Santiago, for his university education and published his first poetry collection when he was nineteen. Between 1927 and 1935, he held a series of honorary consulships around the world, returning to Chile in 1943 to become a senator of the Republic and a member of the Communist Party of Chile. His political interests strongly colored the poetic output of his middle years, though his complete oeuvre, running to several thousand pages, spans a vast range of ideas and passions. He received the Nobel Prize for Literature in 1971. Poems by him appear on pages 32 and 95.

SHARON OLDS (b. 1942) was the New York State poet laureate from 1998 to 2000. She is the author of several volumes of poetry, the second of which, *The Dead and the Living* (1984), won the Lamont Poetry Prize and the National Book Critics Circle Award. She currently holds the chair of New York University's Creative Writing Program. The poet and novelist Michael Ondaatje has said that Olds's poems "are pure fire in the hands—risky, on the verge of failing, and in the end leaping up. I love the roughness and humor and brag and tenderness and completion in her work as she carries the reader through rooms of passion and loss." Poems by her appear on pages 81, 108, and 153.

MARY OLIVER (b. 1935) is one of America's most widely read contemporary poets. The critic Alice Ostriker contends that Oliver is "as visionary as Emerson." She won her first poetry prize at the age of twenty-seven from the Poetry Society of America. She won the Pulitzer Prize in 1984 for her collection of poems, *American Primitive,* and she was a winner of the 1992 National Book Award for Poetry for her *New and Selected Poems.* In an interview for the *Bloomsbury Review* in 1990, she said, "I feel that the function of the poet is to be . . . somehow instructive and opinionated, useful even if only as a devil's advocate. . . . The question asked today is: What does it mean? Nobody says, 'How does it feel?'" Poems by her appear on pages 25, 43, 54, and 173.

GRACE PALEY (b. 1922) is the author of three highly acclaimed collections of short fiction, as well as three volumes of poetry. She has taught at Syracuse and Columbia universities and at Sarah Lawrence College. She has always been actively engaged in the anti-war, feminist, and antinuclear movements. She regards herself as a "somewhat combative pacifist and cooperative anarchist." A poem by her appears on page 155.

FRANCIS PONGE (1899–1988) was a French poet who studied law in Paris and literature in Strasbourg. He had peripheral contacts with the Surrealists in the late twenties, and between the wars he worked as an editor and journalist. An article by Sartre in the early forties praising his work brought him to the public's attention. His poetic method was to observe meticulously and to describe what he saw in rational yet lyrical terms. The result was poems that have been called "verbal still lifes." A poem by him appears on page 157.

RAINER MARIA RILKE (1875–1926) survived a lonely and unhappy childhood in Prague to publish his first volume of poetry in 1894. In 1896 he left Prague for the University of Munich and later made his first trip to Italy and then to Russia. In 1902 in Paris he became friend and secretary to the sculptor Rodin, and the next twelve years in Paris were to see his greatest poetic activity. In 1919 he moved to Switzerland, where he wrote his last two works, *Sonnets to Orpheus* and *Duino Elegies,* in 1923. He died in Switzerland, of leukemia, in 1926. His reputation has grown enormously since his death, and he is now considered one of the greatest poets of the twentieth century. Poems by him appear on pages 42 and 120.

THEODORE ROETHKE (1908–1963) was born in Saginaw, Michigan, to parents who were owners of a local greenhouse. The Great Depression forced Roethke to leave Harvard, where he was taking graduate courses in literature and poetry, and to take up a teaching career. Throughout his life he suffered prolonged bouts of depression, which he consciously used for creative self-exploration through his poetry. His pioneering explorations of nature, regional settings, depth psychology, and personal confessionalism—coupled with his stylistic innovations and mastery of traditional fixed forms—have secured his reputation as one of the most distinguished and highly read American poets of the twentieth century. A poem by him appears on page 70.

RUMI (1207–1273) was the founder of the Sufi order known as the Mevlevi (Whirling Dervishes) in Konya, Turkey. Though the theme of lover and beloved was already established in Sufi teaching, his own poetry was inspired by his meeting and the consequent loss of his great teacher, Shams of Tabriz. Out of their relationship was born some of the most inspired love poetry ever, in which Rumi sings of a love that is both personal and divine at the same time. After Shams's death, Rumi would burst into ecstatic poetry anywhere, anytime, and his scribe and disciple, Husam, was charged with writing it all down. Rumi's great spiritual treatise, *The Math-nawi*, written in couplets, amounts to more than twenty-five thousand lines in six books. Poems by him appear on pages 103 and 116.

ANNE SEXTON (1928–1974) lived in and around Boston all her life and began writing poetry at the age of twenty-nine to keep from killing herself. Language was her lifeline, and somehow—in spite of alcoholism and the mental illness that eventually led her to suicide—she managed to create a body of work that won a Pulitzer Prize. The many Anne Sextons included the 1950s housewife and mother, the seductress, the suicide who carried "kill-me pills" in her handbag, and the poet who made lasting art. A poem by her appears on page 68.

WILLIAM STAFFORD (1914–1993), a native of Kansas, was a poet of ordinary life, and his collected poems are the journal of a man recording his daily experience of living. It was appropriate, then, that he would start each day writing at his desk. For Stafford, the smallest event and the smaller feelings that wash over us could be miracles. His poems are often short and unusually accessible, relying on the power of everyday speech to examine the world. His first major collection of poems, *Traveling Through the Dark*, was published when he was forty-eight and won the National Book Award in 1963. He went on to publish more than sixty-five volumes of poetry and prose, and received many honors and awards. He taught for many years in Oregon. Poems by him appear on pages 44 and 124.

GERALD STERN (b. 1925) was born to immigrant parents in Pittsburgh. He has written poetry all his life, though his first book was not published until he was forty-eight. He claims to have "come from nowhere, and never had any mentors." He has spent his life as a poet and a teacher, having held posts at several American universities. Since his first volume, which received great critical acclaim, he has gone on to publish more than thirteen books, to receive many awards, and to be the first poet laureate of New Jersey. William Mathews has said that Stern is "a poet of ferocious heart and rasping sweetness." Like Whitman, his work is a transformational celebration of the stuff of daily existence. Poems by him appear on pages 50, 148, and 158.

MARK STRAND (b. 1934) was born in Canada and completed his MA at the University of Iowa. He has taught at many universities, including Princeton, Columbia, Harvard, and the University of Utah, where he is now professor of English. He has published several volumes of poetry, and his work is known for a deeply inward sense of language. Octavio Paz wrote of Strand that he "has chosen the negative path, with loss as the first step to fullness; it is also the opening to a transparent verbal perfection." A poem by him appears on page 61.

ANNA SWIR (1900–1984) was the only daughter of an impoverished painter and grew up in his studio in Warsaw, Poland. A militant feminist and author of uninhibited love poems, her work conveys an erotic intensity and warmth, along with an empathy and compassion for those who suffer. Her poems on war and the Nazi occupation of Poland were among the finest of her generation. Czeslaw Milosz and Leonard Nathan have translated her work into English. A poem by her appears on page 56.

WISLAWA SZYMBORSKA (b. 1923) has lived in the city of Krakow, in southern Poland, since 1931. From 1953 to 1981 she was poetry editor for the Krakow literary weekly *Zycie Literackie*. She has written sixteen collections of poetry and has received many honors, including the Nobel Prize for Literature in 1996. Always keen to avoid publicity, she left for a country retreat when news of her Nobel honor reached the media. Though for many years she used a deceptively casual tone to convey her skepticism concerning mankind, her later work is more personal and conveys her belief in the power of words and in the joys arising from the imagination. She has been married twice and has been widowed since the early nineties. Poems by her appear on pages 92 and 161.

DYLAN THOMAS (1914–1953) was the greatest poet that Wales has produced. His father, an English teacher, had him reciting Shakespeare at four years old, and the boy was writing his own poetry by the age of eight. He left school at sixteen and worked for the local newspaper. He moved to London in 1934, and his writing career began to flourish, his first book, *18 Poems,* appearing to rave reviews. During the war, he began a second career as a BBC radio broadcaster. He married and had three children and several affairs. In 1946, with the publication of the collection *Deaths and Entrances,* his popularity exploded. All the while, his drinking and antisocial behavior were becoming out of control. When he came to the United States in 1949 and then again in 1953 to publicize his *Collected Poems,* he was feted by Hollywood and the literary establishment alike. He died in New York of alcohol-related causes. A poem by him appears on page 110.

TOMAS TRANSTRÖMER (b. 1931) is from Stockholm, Sweden, and is the most important Swedish poet since World War II. After several years at the University of Stockholm, he became a psychologist and worked in a center for delinquent youth until the late nineties. His poetry, for which he has received honors from around the world, has been translated into twenty languages. His poems have a great diversity of form and content, and many of them explore the unconscious and challenge the reader's conception of the world. He became known in the United States after Robert Bly translated some of his work in the 1960s. A poem by him appears on page 163.

UVAVNUK (mid-nineteenth to mid-twentieth century) was a shaman of the Inuit tribal people in the northern extremes of North America. It is said that she was struck by lightning, after which she had shamanic powers and dedicated herself to the healing of others. The first translation of *Song of Uvavnuk* was done in the early 1900s. A poem by her appears on page 164.

WALT WHITMAN (1819–1892), of all poets, is America's poet. A journalist and newspaper editor in New York for some years, Whitman was interested in everything, and he was inspired by the vitality of American life and what he saw as the spiritual promise of democracy. He is known above all as the great lover of the sensory and sensual world, and his poems are a constant celebration of life on earth. He self-published the first edition of *Leaves of Grass,* his collected works, in 1855, though it took nearly twenty years and several more editions before it attracted some interest. His colloquial style and free verse emancipated poetry from the conventions of the time, and *Leaves* eventually became a landmark in the history of American letters. A poem by him appears on page 73.

WILLIAM CARLOS WILLIAMS (1883–1963), the son of an English father and a Puerto Rican mother, lived and died in New Jersey. While in medical school at the University of Pennsylvania, he met both Hilda Doolittle and Ezra Pound, the latter remaining a lifelong friend. He was later to say that he could divide his life into "before Pound" and "after Pound." He published his first poetry collection in 1909 while completing his internship in New York City, and Pound found an English publisher for Williams's second volume. He played an active role in the avant-garde poetic movements in Manhattan and aimed to create a specifically American poetics based on the rhythms and colorations of American speech, thought, and experience. His poetry was greatly influenced by his contacts as a doctor with everyday working people. Williams was awarded the Pulitzer Prize a few months after his death. A poem by him appears on page 165.

WILLIAM WORDSWORTH (1770–1850) was born in the Lake District in northern England, and his poetry is suffused with the rugged grandeur and beauty of that region. His mother died when he was eight, and his father died when he was still at school; the sense of being alone in the world is a theme that pervades his work, along with the love and kinship he felt for his sister. He studied at Cambridge, and before his final year, he set out on a walking tour across Europe, which was to profoundly influence his poetic and political sensibilities. His most famous work, *The Prelude*—a book-length autobiographical poem—is considered by many to be the crowning achievement of English romanticism. Though he worked on many versions of it through his lifetime, his wife, Mary, finally published it posthumously in 1850. Poems by him appear on pages 57, 72, and 76.

JAMES WRIGHT (1927–1980) was born in Ohio, graduated from Kenyon College in 1952, and studied in Vienna the following year on a Fulbright scholarship. In 1954 he went to the University of Washington, where he studied with Stanley Kunitz and Theodore Roethke. By the late fifties, he was being published in every important journal and poetry review. In the early sixties, Wright found a kindred spirit in Robert Bly; both of them were interested in a poetry that suggested there were vast powers that awaited release. Wright won many awards, including the Pulitzer for his *Collected Poems*. He continued to write in a manner that was deliberately vulnerable, an extension of the confessional poetry current in the late fifties, yet he transcended the merely personal to reach toward universal and archetypal themes. A poem by him appears on page 166.

W. B. YEATS (1865–1939) was born into the Anglo-Irish landowning class in Dublin, the son of a well-known Irish painter. He was educated in London and Dublin, and became involved in the Celtic Revival, a movement against the cultural influence of English rule. His writing at the turn of the century drew extensively from sources in Irish mythology and folklore. Another potent influence was Maude Gonne, whom he met in 1889. Maude was equally famous for her passionate nationalist politics and her beauty. Though they both married other people, she remained a powerful figure in Yeats's poetry throughout his life. A lifelong fascination for mysticism and the occult is also strongly evident in his work. Yeats is remembered today as one of the greatest poets of the twentieth century. He was awarded the 1923 Nobel Prize for Literature. Poems by him appear on pages 77 and 168.

Permissions Acknowledgments

Index of First Lines

ROGER HOUSDEN, a native of Bath, England, emigrated to the United States in 1998. He now lives in the Bay Area. His books explore existential and cultural issues of our time. His most recent works include *Seven Sins for a Life Worth Living; How Rembrandt Reveals Your Beautiful, Imperfect Self: Life Lessons from the Master; Ten Poems to Last a Lifetime; Ten Poems to Set You Free; Risking Everything: 110 Poems of Love and Revelation; Ten Poems to Open Your Heart; Chasing Rumi: A Fable About Finding the Heart's True Desire;* and *Ten Poems to Change Your Life.*